HARLEY-DAVIDSON MEMORIES

The Golden Age of Motorcycling

HARLEY-DAVIDSON MEMORIES

The Golden Age of Motorcycling

BOB TYSON

TURNER
PUBLISHING COMPANY

Turner Publishing Company

445 Park Avenue, 9th Floor
New York, NY 10022
Phone: (646)291-8961   Fax: (646)291-8962

200 4th Avenue North, Suite 950
Nashville, TN 37219
Phone: (615)255-2665   Fax: (615)255-5081

www.turnerpublishing.com

Harley-Davidson Memories: The Golden Age of Motorcycling

Library of Congress Cataloging-in-Publication Data

Tyson, Bob.
Harley-Davidson memories : the golden age of motorcycling / Bob Tyson.
  p. cm.
ISBN 978-1-63026-352-2
1. Harley-Davidson motorcycle--History. 2. Harley-Davidson Incorporated--History. 3.
Davidson family--History. I. Title.
TL448.H3T97 2010
629.227'509--dc22

2010049038

Printed in the United States of America

10 11 12 13 14 15 16 17 — 0 9 8 7 6 5 4 3 2 1

Contents

Foreword   1

Preface   3

Acknowledgments   9

Introduction   13

1.   Survival of the Fittest   17

2.   Things to Do, Places to Go!   37

3.   Polo Anyone?   67

4.   The Good Old Days   99

5.   Mail Order Motorcycling   139

Foreword

S peaking as a guy who has been collecting and restoring vintage cars and motorcycles for many years, I thought I had seen all the ads, literature, and photos that there were to see, but not so. Author Bob Tyson has put together a treasure trove of family photographs, along with many ads and factory literature that have never been published before, and they are great fun to read and look at. The pictures in this book are the real McCoy, taken by family and relatives enjoying their bikes as they traveled through Maryland and surrounding parts of the East Coast.

Bob's new book, *Harley-Davidson Memories,* is a wonderful nostalgic look back at the joys of motorcycling during what many people have called the Golden Years of Motorcycling. This book hearkens back to an era when men were men, and women were glad of it! It was a time when you had to be a real man to even start one of these machines, much less ride it from one place to another. Remember, nobody had cell phones back then. Motorcycle rides were more of an event that you planned and prepared for, unlike today, when you just get on, push a button, and take off down the road. You had to be more than just a rider; you needed to be a mechanic too! Those were the days!

I know you will enjoy reading this book, and looking back into a great era of American motorcycling history!

Photo by Rick Reed

Preface

There are many of us who fall into the category of motorcycle enthusiasts, young and old, male and female, rich and not so rich, but the one thing we all have in common is that we love motorcycles. Something about the very word *motorcycle* is magical to us. The memories of that first ride are still etched in our minds as if it were yesterday. You can still hear the rumble of the exhaust and feel the wind rushing against your face as you began to believe that you might be the first person ever to feel this wild and free.

As I look back on my own passion for motorcycles, I guess that it all started somewhere around 1964. I was in awe of the big, loud, chrome machines that rode past my house every day. I remember running from the front porch out to the road when I heard them coming. I remember begging one of the neighborhood kids to let me ride his Rupp minibike just so I could pretend it was a motorcycle. I especially remember that fateful day when the father of one of my friends mentioned that he was junking his old "reel" style lawnmower, and told me I could have the engine if I wanted it. I spent weeks rigging that motor up on my three-speed English bike. First the motor mounts, then the exhaust, then the throttle cable, and finally, the minibike clutch bought with money from my paper route. I pestered the local body shop to weld the pedals onto the rear of the frame, so I would have footrests. Finally, I had a machine capable of moving under its own power. That little motorbike would run at speeds up to 35 miles per hour—a flying speed for a twelve-year-old with no fear of traffic or injury. I used the minibike for everything, although I insisted to my dad that I walked it across all roads and only rode it in the woods and fields.

Mom and Dad hated it more than the rock and roll music of the day, and never missed an opportunity to tell me how much trouble I would catch if I got caught riding it on the street. It was the beginning of the end for me. All I thought about was riding my motorbike. I even began to use it on my paper route, much to the dislike of my Sunday morning customers, who were regularly awakened early Sunday morning by the popping of the exhaust from the little Briggs and Stratton motor. Eventually, most of my paper route customers and my neighbors got used to the sight of me flying down the street, pretending to be riding some fully dressed Harley-Davidson.

It was about this time in my life that I realized I was hopelessly addicted to motorcycles and anything connected with them. I hung out around parked motorcycles to talk to the guys who rode them. I scribbled motorcycle names on my school notebooks, and begged a local store owner to take me for a ride on his 1963 Harley-Davidson Duo-Glide. I finally did get caught riding my motorbike without a license, but it only made me want a real motorcycle that much more. My folks said that as long as I lived under their roof, I would not own a bike, and now that my motorbike was safely retired under the porch, I guess they figured the issue would never come up again.

Not too long after that, my best friend, Frank Serio, asked me if I would look after his 1971 Triumph Daytona while he went away to be a soldier. That was the end of the "no motorcycle" rule at my house. From that day on, I followed an endless calendar of swap meets, poker runs, bike shows, and just plain hanging out where motorcycles gathered. I began an almost daily pilgrimage to Daniels, the local biker bar. Even though I had become involved with custom Harleys, my interest was starting to focus more and more on the antique bikes that frequented the bar. Several of the vintage guys even made friends with me, in spite of the 1958 panhead chopper I rode. After a while, it only caught my eye if it was old and rusty. I joined the local chapter of the Antique Motorcycle Club of America, and began my search for my own Holy Grail. The other members in the Chesapeake Chapter assured me that all the bikes had been found, and I promptly found one a year for several years, usually by accident. Which is the very way I stumbled upon the photos in this book, by complete accident, and just being in the right place at the right time.

The King of Packrats

If you look up the word *packrat* in Webster's dictionary, you will likely see a picture of my father, just above my own photo. He saved the tie wires from loaves of bread, if you get my meaning. But if it weren't for my dad's fondness for saving things I might never have found these photos. My father was almost totally deaf, a result of working around aircraft during World War II without the benefit of hearing protection. This made even casual conversation difficult at best, but by talking loudly, and reading lips, we managed to communicate. One particular Saturday afternoon in 1988, I stopped by to visit my mom and dad, and catch up on what was going on in the family. My father beckoned me outside so we could converse without disturbing my mom, as the "conversation" can be quite loud trying to get my dad to understand what I'm saying. As we stood in the front yard shouting our family gossip back and forth, Dad noticed my mom's Aunt Doris exiting her house across the street carrying a large brightly wrapped box in her arms. We then both watched in amusement as Aunt Doris attempted to force this rather large box into a standard sized trash can.

Finally, Dad could take the suspense no longer, and called over to her to ask what was in the box. She replied that she had just finished cleaning out the attic, and the box was full of old family negatives that were no longer of interest to her. Naturally, my dad couldn't hear a word she said and turned to me for the answer. "Pictures Dad, just old pictures" I said, as he took off across the street to retrieve the box. My father thought the odds were good that some of the photos in the box would picture my mom's side of the family, and might be worth a look. Aunt Doris was only too happy to have someone else take the box off her hands, and eagerly handed it over. When he returned with the box and opened it up, he was disappointed to find that it contained dozens of yellowed envelopes full of large format negatives. That's when he decided maybe it wasn't such a good find after all. I was prepared to return them to the trash can myself, when I thought I should have a quick peek at what they depicted. By chance the very first envelope I pulled out had "Motorcycle Hill Climb-1919" penciled on it, and I stood there, holding the negatives up to the sun to have a better look.

Dad smiled at me as I put the box in my truck, as if he knew that the desire to save things was genetically passed on. Aunt Doris was thrilled to see the photos after they were printed, and was kind enough to revive the memories of who the subjects were, and when and where they were photographed. I took notes and talked to other family members who could remember these adventurous ancestors, and even got my dad to admit not only that he had always liked motorcycles, but that he had once owned an Indian Four.

What follows in this book combines the photographs saved from my Aunt Doris's trash can, photos from my own collection, and contributions from friends and members of the Chesapeake Chapter of the AMCA, with old advertisements, catalogs, newspaper clippings, and other items I have kept over the years, about my favorite thing in the whole world—motorcycles.

Acknowledgments

I have to thank some special friends who helped me along with this book project. First, my good friends Ken Watson and Dave Panella, for lighting the fires of interest in antique motorcycles and weaning me away from the custom bikes and choppers that I always rode. They did this by letting me ride practically everything they owned at one time or another, and I will always appreciate those rides!

My longtime friend Tom Finn, who suggested that I try getting my book published. Even after two publishers rejected me, I kept trying until the project was picked up, because I knew that someone thought it was a great project. Tom has always helped me when

I asked him, and that's what friendship is all about.

Scott English, for the loan of some nice original ad copy and photos from his family's album, and taking the time to introduce me to his aunt, Mrs. Virginia Forrer, who was quite the motorcyclist in her own right, and was gracious enough to tell me her stories.

Plummer Wiley, for lending me his scrapbook of literature, photos, and personal documents from his college days from 1930 through 1934. He was an amazing individual, and I was proud to know him.

Keith Ball, the editor of *Easyriders Magazine,* for helping me leave the ranks of the completely unpublished, and giving me the "Baltimore Bob" nickname!

Dr. Martin Jack Rosenblum, for his time, his comments, and for being such a great inspiration.

Willie G. Davidson, for allowing me to interrupt his day and taking time to look through my photograph collection. He convinced me of what a wonderful batch of photos I had.

Milby Jones, a great friend and fellow machinist and motorcycle enthusiast, he became like a second father to me, and helped me with many projects over the years. Milby was truly a legend in the antique motorcycle community.

Lisa, and the gang at Severn Graphics, for all their help and patience.

Jay Leno, one of the best-known faces in both entertainment and the hobby of motorcycling, was gracious enough to write my foreword. I am honored to know him, and very appreciative that he took an interest in my project.

Most of all, I wish to thank my wife, Kathy, and my son, Matthew, for tolerating my work on this project for several years, and allowing my little piles of photos and papers all over the house!

—Bob Tyson

Introduction

Welcome to *Harley-Davidson Memories,* a unique and personal glimpse back into the Golden Years of motorcycling. Turn these pages and take a trip back in time as you see how the bikers before us did what we all love to do, ride motorcycles. This book is not another technical history, because that has been done many times before, and I don't think I could add anything, or do it better than it has been done before. Nor is it a book full of staged factory publicity photos, like you may be used to seeing in every other Harley-Davidson history. This book is a scrapbook of real people, doing real things with their own motorcycles. Road trips, picnics, Jack Pine Enduros, and family vacations are all captured here on film in a time when photography was still something of a novelty itself. Yet one look at these photos will tell you that the photographer had a great eye for a nice picture as well as a love for the machines. Not only was he a photographer, but he was an avid motorcyclist, and he knew exactly what images he wanted to save for future enthusiasts to see.

Many people refer to the period between 1915 and 1930 as "the Golden Age of Motorcycling." Hundreds of different machines graced the countryside, with something new and different on each and every one of them. Taking a ride was like going on an adventure, never knowing what the trip would bring. Navigation of rural roads was a challenge, and one hoped he had enough fuel to make it back home. Clubs formed, riders gathered for enduros and hill-climbs, and national organizations helped protect the motorcyclist's rights. People discovered a vehicle that was able to transport them from one place to another just as it simultaneously refreshed the soul of the rider. It was freedom in the shape of two wheels, as America began its love affair with the motorcycle.

You will notice that quite a few of the motorcycles bear the same name, Harley-Davidson. There is a good reason for that. By virtue of their superior products, a conservative business approach, and a very strong dealer network, Harley-Davidson managed to endure while scores of other makes quietly slipped away, never to be heard from again. After the Schwinn company pulled out of the motorcycle business by ceasing production of their Excelsior Henderson line, only the Indian Motorcycle Company remained as any real competition for Harley-Davidson. And while Indian riders were full of the same fierce loyalty and devotion to their mounts as Harley riders, a long series of bad management decisions finally caused Indian to go out of business in 1953.

There are a few other makes shown in this book, as evidence of the more than two hundred other brands built in America from 1900 up to the time of the Great Depression. Some of the photos are all that remain of these wonderful machines. Harley-Davidson Memories is more than just another book with motorcycle photos in it. It is a celebration of the machines and the people who rode them and loved them, and for a while at least, held on to a piece of their own Harley-Davidson memories.

Live to ride, and ride safe!

The Only Force
he respects

1
Survival of the Fittest

The first thing one may notice about this book is the abundance of one particular brand of motorcycle in the photographs. That brand is Harley-Davidson, the one manufacturer that managed to outlast all the others while becoming a legend in the process. If only the four founders could see the results of their humble beginnings. Would they ever believe they created a machine so charismatic and powerful, that people would be compelled to have that machine's name tattooed on their bodies? A product so rebellious that it would become an entire lifestyle for many? This is the amazing story of success for the lone survivor of a once crowded market. Harley-Davidson celebrated their 100th anniversary in the year 2003. Now, we can take a look back at what made them a survivor and an American legend.

When Bill Harley and his pal Arthur Davidson started tinkering with the idea of engine assisted cycling in 1901, they probably had no idea where it would lead them. All they really wanted to do was try to take some of the work out of riding a bicycle, by using some of the early technology available to them at that time. Both-

This photo only hints at the wide variety of choices that the motorcyclist had in the early 1900s. The number of motorcycle manufacturers in the United States alone approached 300 at the peak of cycling popularity, around the year 1912. Most were very poorly made, and quickly faded away, but many were solid, well-engineered machines with outstanding features and performance. Even that, however, didn't always guarantee longevity, and in the end, only Indian and Harley-Davidson made it past the post-Depression years. On the far left is a 1911 Yale 61-cubic-inch twin, made in Toledo, Ohio, by the Consolidated Manufacturing Company, which bought out the fledgling California Motorcycle Company in 1902. Yale ended their motorcycle production in 1915. The next machine is a 1912 Indian 61-cubic-inch twin. This bike was rated at 7 horsepower, with a top speed of 55 m.p.h. Next in line is a 1912 Harley-Davidson belt drive single, displacing almost 500 cc. This bike is the only one shown here equipped with lighting. Second from the right is a Thor motorcycle, built in Illinois by the Aurora Automatic Machinery Company. Aurora was contracted to supply engines for the first Indian motorcycles while the Springfield plant was still young, and they eventually went on to market their own Thor line of motorcycles between 1901 and 1919. The identity of the last bike is unclear, but due to the configuration of the forks and handlebars, it appears to be another Thor machine.

men worked for the same Milwaukee firm during the day while they spent evenings together engaged in work on their motorcycle designs.

Bill Harley was employed as a draftsman, and he had quite a bit of experience with building bicycles prior to his drafting job. Arthur Davidson worked as a pattern maker, which gave him the knowledge to build patterns for the castings of a small gasoline engine that he and Bill were experimenting with.

They were friends with a German draftsman at the company who knew a few things about the DiDeon engines used in early European motorbikes. Some of this knowledge he shared with the two men. The project moved slowly ahead, and with the use of a friend's lathe and other small machinery, the parts began to come together. Every free moment was spent working on the new machine. Around this time, Arthur's brother Walter came back to Milwaukee from his employment as a railroad machinist in Kansas for the wedding of another Davidson brother. He became so excited with Bill and Arthur's motorcycle project that he decided to stay in Milwaukee. The enthusiasm was contagious! The three men slowly overcame one obstacle at a time while refining their machine. At that time in America, there was little practical information available on the subject of gasoline engines, and the many systems involved in the operation of one. Ignition components were crude, and working carburetion was almost unheard of. Most engine parts were made or machined by hand in the tiny workshop. After some time, a third Davidson brother, William, joined in the pursuit for a better mode of transportation.

The year had slipped into 1903, and the nation was eager for new ideas and inventions. Elsewhere in the country, two brothers were putting the finishing touches on their gas engine powered glider, while another gentleman was testing his automobile in the suburbs of Detroit. Up in Springfield, Massachusetts, two men were already in production of their small yet robust motorcycle, which they called the Indian, after the pioneer spirit of young America. It was, as many history books would later note, a milestone year for transportation advances.

Bill Harley and the Davidson brothers weren't the only ones trying to come up with a more powerful, dependable motorcycle that would last. There were many inventors and mechanics across the country doing exactly the same thing. What was it that made their machine different? What gave them the magic formula to outlast all the rest? How did their fledgling company survive some of the toughest times in America's history? To answer these questions, a person need only look at how the four men went about solving the problems they encountered as they designed and built their machine.

From the very beginning, they were committed to building a machine capable of withstanding use on the rough Wisconsin roads around them. They all agreed that there could be no easy way to do this. This machine must be the best they could make it, or it was back to the drawing board for them. Each and every obstacle was overcome by methodically working out the problem, until the correct solution was found. Finally they were ready to test the bike. After road testing the machine, the founders realized that the engine was under-powered, and the frame was not strong enough. Rather than give up, or settle for poor performance, they went back to work with renewed vigor. The engine displacement was increased substantially, and the frame was redesigned as a loop style, dedicated for motorcycle use, and not a modification of a weak bicycle frame. This effort at considerable improvement

Together as if they were always destined to be rivals, these two brands would out-last all the others during the Golden Era of motorcycling. Both Indian and Harley-Davidson motorcycles were well-built, well-engineered machines, and gave their owners all that was promised to them. Here some farm folks check out the latest in powered transportation sometime in 1912. The Indian machine is a 61-cubic-inch v-twin, rated at 7 horsepower. Magneto ignition was standard in 1912, and this bike would have been a single-speed model. The two-speed hub was introduced the following year. The 380-pound bike was capable of speeds exceeding 50 miles per hour. The single cylinder Harley-Davidson is a Model 8A, also with magneto ignition. This engine still used the suction type intake valve, and produced 4.34 horsepower. The so-called Silent Gray Fellow was aptly named for both its efficient exhaust system, and the color scheme it used. By 1912, Harley-Davidson had established a reputation for dependable machines.

was typical of these four men's approach to building the perfect motorcycle.

The new design proved to be a success, and the Harley-Davidson Motor Company was in business. Their first production motorcycle was paid for before it was completed, and delivered to a Mr. Meyer, who racked up almost six thousand miles before selling it. The second buyer, a gentleman named George Lyon, added another fifteen thousand miles on the machine. The Motor Company promptly began two more machines, which were completed in 1904. According to Motor Company history, both 1904 bikes were paid for up front, which says something about the confidence

A typical gathering of riders at Rupp's Harley-Davidson dealership, in southern Pennsylvania around 1928. Dealers became a meeting place for groups of motorcycle enthusiasts who favored the Milwaukee brand. It was this type of rider loyalty that made Harley-Davidson's dealer network so strong, especially in the post-Depression years, when new bike sales were at an all time low. Dealers like this one encouraged riders to bring their older machines in for rebuilds and maintenance to keep bikes running during tough economic times. Note the popularity of aviator-style goggles, a reminder that motorcycling and flying have a lot in common!

that the Davidson brothers and Bill Harley instilled in customers. It didn't take long before other inquiries came in for machines to be built. Word spread quickly of the reliable motorcycles these four men were building. By now, the motorcycle venture was demanding more and more time from the young men, and it was time to totally commit to the project. It was decided that Bill Harley would attend the University of Wisconsin to study engineering while the Davidson brothers continued developing the business. This decision illustrates the kind of long-range thinking that separated Harley-Davidson from their competitors. Bill Harley knew that in order to learn cutting-edge gasoline engine technology in 1904, he would have to study with people more experienced than he was. The science of gasoline engines was still in its very early stages, and there were many different opinions on what worked and what didn't. Harley-Davidson tended to stay with the tried and true methods, a trademark that worked well for them over the next few years. They took great pride in advertising the fact that Harley-Davidsons were made with the best materials available. Their reputation was respected in the motorcycling community, and their machines became known for reliability and quality. The Motor Company printed their first sales brochure in 1906, which stated with complete confidence that "no other motorcycles except special racing machines can pass them either on the hills or on the level." Perhaps this was the beginning of Harley-Davidson's unbeatable legend.

Bill Harley and the Davidson brothers also knew that a strong dealer network was key to staying on top of the motorcycle game.

It wasn't enough to build a good machine. In order to be successful as a manufacturer, they knew they would need to keep in touch with riders all over the world who would give their products the ultimate test. They needed to have dealers committed to service and selling Harley-Davidson motorcycles and repair parts. It was Arthur Davidson who quickly became the salesman of the four founders. He began his recruitment of dealers in America sometime during 1910. This was no easy task during a time when many other motorcycle companies were trying hard to sell their machines to the same dealers that Harley-Davidson was attempting to win over. At this early stage in the company's development, the only claim to fame H-D had was the Federation of American Motorcyclists Award for a perfect score in the New York state endurance run in 1908. Brother Walter Davidson was at the controls for this event, and was one of sixty-one entrants. He rode the only Harley-Davidson machine in the field of competitors, and was not expected to finish. His win may have been a big factor in the company's early success. Beyond question, this one single event had a huge impact on the Motor Company's future, and Harley-Davidson solidified its place in motorcycling history.

Riders confidently bought Harley-Davidson machines because they knew anywhere they went across the United States, a dealer would be close by to help them if they needed it. While we think nothing of a 100-mile trip today, an early cyclist had to feel good about his machine, or conclude that his chances of returning home without mechanical failure were less than robust. An entire lifestyle began to emerge through motorcycling, and through Harley-

Davidson dealers. They became places to hang out, talk shop about bikes, meet your chums, or get service for your machine. Dealers took on the role of the "general store" to their customers. H-D has rekindled this kind of camaraderie in recent years with the formation of its Harley Owners Group factory-sponsored club, affectionately known as "H.O.G."

Motorcycling could include friends, too! With the addition of a sidecar, or a tandem seat for the solo machine, two could enjoy a ride together. Sidecar-equipped motorcycles actually cost more than a Model T Ford, even though operating costs were substantially less for the motorcycle. This made it difficult for a family man to justify a sidecar rig with a growing family to transport. H-D offered standard-width sidecars, and two-passenger models for a slight extra cost. Some states even required a separate license tag for the sidecar in addition to the tag required for the motorcycle. In 1920, Maryland was one such state. These bikes are all 61-cubic-inch J model twins.

A group of riders pose near one of their machines, exhibiting their good taste in motorcycling clothing. Gentlemen of the day were eager to get involved with the adventurous sport of motorcycling, yet most took great pride in their appearance as motorcyclists. Harley-Davidson dealers marketed quite a lot of riding clothes and accessories, much like the "motor clothes" offered at dealers today. A closer look at the bike shows the gauntlet-style gloves attached to the handlebars for cold weather riding. These gauntlets were a very popular item for cyclists, since most early cyclists rode their machines year round. The leggings on the rider at right are known as puttees, and typically were made of reinforced leather. They kept oil and road dirt from the rider's pants, as well as kept the pant legs from getting caught in belt pulleys and the like. This photo was taken in 1915.

Harley-Davidson appealed to the outdoorsman in most men to come enjoy the sport of motorcycling. Whether that meant a ride in the country, or a trip into the city, it made no difference so long as one could be on a bike. This freedom was appealing to people used to pedaling, walking, or riding a horse and carriage to get places.

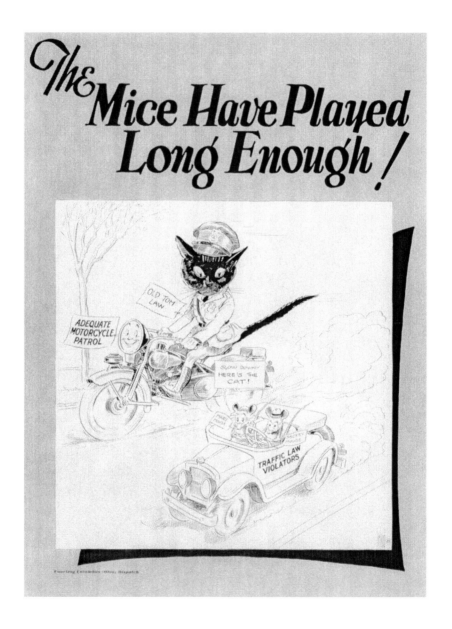

Something tells me that these folks weren't the actual riders of this beautiful 1916 Henderson. White clothing didn't stay white very long on a four-cylinder bike with exposed valve assemblies. Even in 1916, Henderson had a reputation for dependable, powerful motorcycles. The machine was built in Detroit, at the Henderson Motor Company, which was started in 1912 by brothers Tom and William Henderson. They later sold the company to Ignatz Schwinn, who moved the factory to Chicago, and eventually went out of the motorcycle business in 1931. William Henderson went on to design and build four-cylinder machines under the ACE name, until he was killed in a traffic accident in 1922 while testing one of his own machines.

Close-up of Buddy Seat. Fits in place of saddle. Is upholstered in sponge rubber, covered with water-proof cowhide. Note hand holds and extension on footboards. Auxiliary spring is used when carrying extra passenger.

The "Buddy Seat"... /
the New Saddle for Two,

"A soldier bluff with a little bit of fluff
on a winter afternoon."
—"The Bystander," November 10, 1915

The Book of "The Silent Grey" post free from

HARLEY-DAVIDSON MOTOR CO., LTD
33 Harleyson House, Newman Street, London, W

50 MOTORCYCLE EQUIPMENT CO. MECO HAMMONDSPORT, N.Y.
LOS ANGELES, CAL.

MID-WEST STORAGE BATTERY

Price $15.00 Prepaid

The Mid-West organization builds high grade storage batteries for motorcycles exclusively. Their product is the result of careful engineering and quality workmanship and all the material used in the construction of these batteries is chosen with the idea of giving the most dependable service to the user. They are of very high capacity thus allowing the rider to make use of additional lights and will also stand up for a long period under the wear and tear incidental to motorcycle usage. On the basis of a quality product at a fair price we recommend Mid-West's to you.

These batteries are built for all models of electrically equipped motorcycles. Each type is built as a complete replacement and will fit the motorcycle container with the same exactness as to connections and all other details as does the original equipment.

Type No. 1635—Fits Excelsior, Henderson, Reading Standard and Ace.
Type No. 2635—Fits all electrically equipped Harley Davidsons.
Type No. 4635—Fits all electrically equipped Indians except 1914.

MOTORCYCLE WINDSHIELD
No. M181—$8.50

This windshield is strong and well made and will give your motorcycle an attractive and finished appearance. Made of water-proof, rubber-finished cloth stretched over a metal frame. The window is of good weight celluloid. Can be quickly attached to or detached from your motorcycle.

No one would drive an automobile without a windshield. The motorcyclist needs this same protection even more as he usually travels at a higher rate of speed than the average automobile. Shipped prepaid within the fifth zone only.

COMBINATION MOTORCYCLE LOCK
No. F17—$1.15

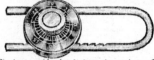

The best combination lock on the market. Positively cannot be opened except on the four turn combination which you will receive with the lock. No keys to bother with or get lost. Nickel plated. Shackle is 7½ in. long.

COMBINATION PADLOCK
No. F9—$1.00

The same lock as shown above but with shackle of ordinary length. Everyone has use for a lock and if anything is worth putting any kind of a lock on, it is worth putting a **good** lock on. We here offer you the best for the price.

MECO MOTORCYCLE LOCK
No. F19   95c

Your motorcycle is not safe without a lock. Here is a good one at a low price. The shackle is long enough to lock over the forks through the wheel.

FINGER NAIL CLIPPER
No. A4E
Now 20c

A handy pocket utensil.

A useful article often sold for 25c.

CLOVER COMPOUND
2 Cans in One—Coarse and Fine
No. F21—30c per Box

A quick valve grinding compound. Don't fuss with slow emery. Use this and do a quick, smooth job. Enough for several seasons.

AUTOMOBILES
KILL MORE
THAN CRIMINALS

2
Things to Do, Places to Go!

Bikers—Then and Now

Nowadays, whenever we feel the need to refresh our spirits on our bike, it's no big deal to roll our machine out of the garage, turn on the ignition, push the starter button (for those who don't remember the kick thing), and head down the road, without a care in the world. In the early days of motorcycling, it wasn't quite that easy. What did the novice biker need in the early 1900s? Let's start with the main ingredient necessary to go for a ride—a motorcycle. Finding more than one manufacturer around 1919 was not a problem, as there were well over one hundred companies building bikes. Finding one that lived up to its promises was the hard part.

For the sake of argument, let's say you read the trade magazines, you talked to others who rode different brands, and you decided, as you might today, that Harley-Davidson made a pretty good machine. It's a safe bet that there was no two-year waiting list in 1919, unlike today, so hopefully you could just find a dealer in your area and walk in to buy a bike. Harley-Davidson's founders believed very early on that a strong and well-represented dealer network was essential to staying alive in a very competitive field. That was one of the reasons that Harley-Davidson was able to

Motorcycles lost their hold on Americans when automobiles became cheaper, and more practical as transportation. Especially for the family man, a car would carry more, and provide much more comfort than a motorcycle. That didn't stop the adventurous from taking a chance on owning one, though. Here a young man takes a ride in the park on a beautiful summer day, while an automobile crosses the stone bridge behind him. Traffic control was left to those willing to share the roads with other vehicles, and could be a dangerous endeavor. The bike is a 1920 Harley-Davidson.

survive some of the worst economic times that came their way in later years. They laid the groundwork early on for a strong, loyal dealer network, and it paid off as time went on. So, in the early days, how would you pay for your bike? Actually, just like today, you could pay as you rode with a finance plan arranged by the factory. According to company historians, Kilborne Finance Company of Milwaukee offered a credit plan for those who didn't have enough money to buy a bike. Eventually, many of Harley-Davidson's dealers were able to extend this incentive to their prospective customers.

Let's say you bought a nice "J" model twin. What then? Typically, the dealer would give you a few minutes of instruction for the starting sequence of the machine, and maybe some idea of what the controls did, then point you down the road, and you were on your way. This may sound a little silly, but it was probably closer to the truth than you may think. Many first-time riders made their decisions whether or not to continue riding largely by the success or failure of their first ride. Dropping a machine was called "unloading," and not something you wanted to do with your own or someone else's bike.

The dealer showed you how to give the motor a shot of oil with the hand pump located on the top of the gas tank, and how to turn back the spark advance to start the bike, and maybe you had to use the compression release to lift the front cylinder exhaust valve off its seat. This allowed you to spin the engine over a little easier, especially if it was a cold day. You might find that kicking over the engine was harder than you expected, but this machine was a

61-cubic-inch model, and it took a little persuasion. If the kicker wouldn't engage, you had to step down on a little plunger on the side of the transmission to mesh the starter gears before you could kick again. Then you might want to put the choke on and kick through once or twice to prime the engine. On a really cold day, you'd have to inject some gasoline into each cylinder to prime them through the priming cocks, located at the top side of each cylinder. Wow! There was more to it than meets the eye, wasn't there? And then, as the rider's handbook said, "just turn on ignition key, and start motor with vigorous strokes of the starter." Some technical writer must have had a good laugh with that part!

In the Beginning

In the early 1900s, motorized transportation did more to change America than any other single invention. Suddenly, farmers had the mobility to run into town from twenty miles away and make it home the same day, and city folks could jump on their very own engine-assisted cycle to ride out through the countryside. After years and years of horse and wagon, or just plain horses, and slowly graduating to the bicycle, here was the answer everyone had been waiting for. In today's fast-paced world, it may be difficult to imagine a time without motor vehicles, but at the turn of the century, the horse and buggy was a reality for most Americans. For the farmer living out in the middle of nowhere, going into town was a planned event, and not something one did on the spur of the moment. Some early motorcycle manufacturers were quick to use this fact in their advertising, as they pointed out to the farmer the advantages of having a vehicle capable of saving plenty of time going to or from the nearest town.

The Indian Motorcycle Company was one of the first to advertise in this manner. Their ad campaign stated that every farm should have an Indian on it. Maybe even an Indian with a sidecar, so the wife and kids could ride along to town, or just to tour the countryside on Sundays. Indian ads also mentioned that the sidecar was very useful for delivering produce from the farm, or bringing home that important merchandise to keep the farm running.

Only one guess as to which manufacturer wrote this ad! Indian claimed that "motocycles" really were safer than automobiles, but where did they get the 1/3 of a percent?

Harley-Davidson, on the other hand, ran ads telling farmers to buy a motorcycle for their most important employee on the farm, the son of the owner. The ads during the First World War claimed that because of the labor shortage from the war, a practical thing to do would be to buy a time-saving motorcycle that could also be used for pleasure. Harley-Davidson tended to stay with such practical and conservative approaches in their ads, and their business. While many of the other brands took on a flashy, almost boastful image, H-D stayed with the tried and true method of accurately describing their machines, even if the facts sometimes sounded like bragging. The Motor Company was justifiably proud of its National Endurance Contest win in 1908, with the one-thousand-plus-five-point score, and often said so in its ads.

It is apparent from early ads that motorcycles were looked upon as more than just transportation. They were also marketed as essential work equipment. As the motorized revolution began to

The combination of women and motorcycles goes back quite awhile, even for the rural folks. In 1922, these farm girls were probably feeling special to even be photographed on these new machines. The bikes are 1922 model J twins, which had 74-cubic-inch motors with battery ignition. This engine first became available a year earlier in 1921, and was rated at 8.68 horsepower through a three-speed transmission. Both machines were also equipped with electric lighting and auxiliary passenger seats, commonly called tandems. The bike on the right had a seat backrest for the operator, which had to be a nice accessory on long trips. Close inspection of the bikes reveals that the rear fender was not hinged, a feature that was introduced in 1923, allowing easier removal of the rear wheel on the rear stand. These two machines were among the almost 13,000 motorcycles built by Harley-Davidson in 1922, up from 10,000 in 1921. One of the big changes for H-D this year was the introduction of the new brewster green with gold striping, replacing the olive green used from 1917 through 1921.

invade American farms in the shape of tractors, harvesting equipment, and other engine-assisted devices, farmers were finding the motorcycle to be a tool that was just as useful. According to some early Motor Company records, in certain parts of the country, 1 out of 8 farmers owned a motorcycle in 1911, and most were Harley-Davidsons. No doubt some of the farmers who used motorcycles had a hard time hiding the smile on their faces as they whizzed down the dirt road to town. Who said farming couldn't be fun?

Rural mail delivery services were quick to make use of the motorcycle in keeping their appointed rounds. Some of the subcontracted special delivery messengers got paid a percentage of the mail charges, and usually had a certain time period in which to deliver the packages or mail to the recipient. These messengers were also expected to have their own vehicle, and to some, the obvious choice was the motorcycle. A sidecar could hold quite a bit of mail, and the operating costs for a motorcycle were much cheaper than those for an automobile. Motorcycles also ate a lot less than the horses previously used for mail delivery. In 1922, the United States Post Master issued a special delivery Harley-Davidson stamp to recognize the special delivery messengers, known as "Speedy." Not long afterward, sometime in the mid-1920s, the U.S. Post Office put an end to the use of motorcycles for mail delivery, owing to an increasing number of accidents.

Not all things dealing with motorcycles had to involve work. By the late teens and early twenties, the emphasis was beginning to shift from transportation to more casual references to sporting. Harley-Davidson's ads said "Motorcycling is the greatest sport on wheels!" and that "motorcycling is the sport of sports"! Manufacturers tried to appeal to the "red-blooded outdoors man" in every American by extolling the virtues of riding through the countryside on a powerful machine capable of going far and wide without worry of mechanical failure. In reality, the ads painted a much prettier picture than actually existed. Even though the League of American Wheelmen had made great improvements in city roads during the heyday of the bicycle, country roads and lanes were a far cry from the smooth-paved roads in the cities. A good rain turned most country roads into quagmires of varying depth, often virtually impassable by automobile or motorcycle. For this reason many early sidecar rigs had adjustable wheel track width on the sidecar. This enabled the rider to change his wheel width to match that of the wagons or autos that had gone before him down a muddy or rutted country road. Harley-Davidson equipped their "J" model twins with a hand lever attached to the foot clutch linkage, to allow the rider of a sidecar-fitted machine to walk beside his rig in the event of muddy roads or deep sand.

On the Road Again

On your bike of yesteryear, you've mastered the art of starting the machine, and getting it in gear and under way without too much difficulty, but what now? How about a nice ride in the country, maybe a spin to Uncle Dwight's farm for a visit. It's only fifteen miles one way, and you should be able to handle that. Better make sure you've got plenty of gas first. The tank looks a little low, so maybe you'd better pull into the first gas station you see. But wait, there are no gas stations! The first gas station didn't open in the United States until 1912, in Los Angeles. Where do you go for fuel? The general hardware store in town will sell you some gas at 10 to 15 cents a gallon, but you will have to pump it out of a drum behind the store.

You have now filled the tank, and made sure you have plenty of oil in the oil tank, so you're off to visit Uncle Dwight. If you happen to run out of gasoline in the countryside, you had better hope that some kind farmer has a gas can or two on the farm for keeping his gas-powered tractor running; otherwise, you may wind up pushing your machine back to town.

This photo is what motorcycling is all about. A sunny day, a gravel road through the mountains, and a dependable machine underneath you. The rider is standing next to a 1922 or 1923 J model twin. The rear tire is excessively worn, which must have made for cautious riding on gravel. The bike bears a 1923 Maryland tag, so it's fairly safe to assume that the model year is 1922.

A fifteen-mile trip could be a big adventure for the novice motorcyclist in the early teens, because one never knew what might happen on the road. Around the next turn might be a mud pit, or even a flock of sheep. Keep in mind that most of these roads were nothing more than dirt lanes, barely wide enough for one wagon

The position of the headlight below the horn identifies this machine as a 1918 J model twin. The engine displacement was 61 cubic inches, and the horsepower output was rated at 8.6 hp. Ignition was controlled by magneto, with a mechanically operated circuit breaker, replacing the vacuum unit of the previous years. Also new for 1918 was the lubrication access hole in the primary cover, allowing the rider to grease the clutch without having to take everything apart. The proud rider of this machine is wearing typical attire for a motorcyclist of the day, including the stiff leggings, called puttees, and he follows the practice of turning his cap around so the wind won't catch the brim. Goggles for eye protection on dusty roads were another necessity for the early motorcyclist. This bike has an auxiliary seat with floorboards for the passenger, and even has a tire pump mounted on the front downtube of the frame. This pump, along with a tire patch kit, was a very handy item to have on unpaved roads.

or vehicle to pass through, and there was always the chance of encountering another motorist heading the other direction. Traffic control was unheard of in the rural areas, which meant no lights, no paved roads, and no stop signs. There were no road signs either. You had to navigate by landmarks or directions from the locals if you didn't know which way to go. Sounds a lot like the trips I usually take on my bike! Don't forget to pack a couple of spare inner tubes, or a tire patch kit!

Farmers and Bikers

One of the less-publicized accessories that came with motorcycle ownership was the instant and sometimes unkind wrath of other members of the wheeled public. In spite of all the manufacturers' ads that proclaimed the joy of country rides on your motorcycle, none of the ads bothered to go into detail about the rules of sharing the road with the inhabitants of these rural areas. Imagine being a farmer, and perhaps moving your herd across the dirt lane from one pasture to another, when all of a sudden around the bend comes a speeding motorcyclist. His engine, popping and revving loudly, scatters your herd all over the place, while he zooms by with a wicked grin on his face! It only took a few instances like this to help create an image that is still attached to motorcycles and their riders to this day. Newspaper cartoonists took regular shots at these early motorcyclists and their newfangled machines, by making jokes about the laws that were enacted to "curb" the unruly riders. Many towns posted speed limit signs especially for motorcycles, while allowing automobiles to proceed without interference. Is it any wonder we wound up with such a bad boy image?

Harley-Davidson worked hard at changing the public's view of motorcycles. From early on, it decried the practice of running a motorcycle with an open or straight exhaust pipe, and maintained that Harley-Davidson motorcycles were very quiet, dependable machines. This reputation for smooth, quiet machines earned Harley-Davidson motorcycles the nickname "the Silent Gray Fellow." Harley ads claimed that their machine was so silent that it could not be heard across the street. They never stated how wide that street was!

Women riders were not a common sight in the 1920s and 1930s, but some dared to break with tradition and enjoy themselves just as the guys did. Janet Thompson was one such woman, and her ride of choice was a Henderson four-cylinder machine, believed to be a 1925 Model K. At 450 pounds, this was a big and heavy machine for a woman to ride, but she logged many miles in the New England area. A bike like this one could easily run 80 miles per hour.

The Delaware River Bridge, around 1925. Baltimore cyclist George Hoffman sees nothing wrong with stopping in the middle of the bridge to take this photograph of his Model JD Harley-Davidson while his mother-in-law waits patiently in the sidecar. Take notice of the "Baltimore" pennant hanging from the back of the sidecar.

How to find fun, sport, health and happiness in 13 easy lessons.

Always ride a motorcycle is perhaps the most important lesson. Leastwise, it fits in very well here.

Ride away from the every day humdrum of existence. Go places — get there and back!

Leave your worries at home. This is easy — very easy — with a motorcycle.

Everybody's taking to the open road. You can too, and enjoy it MORE, with a motorcycle.

Your motorcycle is a means of transportation and sport, and an outlet for that "boxed up" feeling.

— * * * * *

Don't let the skeptic get your goat. Remember. one ride in a sidecar is usually enough to convince the most obstinate. (Apologies to Frank.)

A motorcycle, a tank of gasoline and oil are all that's needed. Then the highways and byways spell "FREEDOM".

Very, very many advocates believe that OUR sport is the king of ALL sports. They're right, too.

Into the hills, through the valleys, along cool streams we glide. Fellows, this is the life!

Do your part to boost the best there is in motorcycling. This helps all of us — lots.

Sunny days are all there is. There is no gloom where there is a motorcyclist.

On, on! Your motorcycle will take you wherever your heart desires.

Now, we didn't mention any particular brand of motorcycle, did we? Well, it isn't hard to figure out the brand we have in mind!

An alley in East Baltimore, behind Riggs Avenue, where one of these riders lived in 1922, became a photo opportunity, and a chance to clown around for the camera. Owning these Harley-Davidson machines was somewhat of a luxury in a working-class neighborhood like this one, when many people still got around by bicycle or horse and carriage.

If not for the photographer, this could be a scene in part of a typical ride in the countryside—broken down on a dirt road in the middle of nowhere, with only a few hand tools to repair the machine. The ruts on the side of the road are evidence to what happened on dirt roads after a heavy rain. They became extremely difficult to navigate on a solo machine, and sometimes the added weight of a sidecar rig would work to the rider's disadvantage. Try to imagine coming around this curve at 40 miles an hour with a very worn front tire! The machine appears to be a 1917 Harley-Davidson J model twin.

This is one of my favorite shots, just because it sums up the universal appeal of motorcycle riding. A beautiful day, two fellas with their girlfriends, and two exciting machines, ready to take them anywhere they want to go. Besides, you gotta love the hats!

Merle Batts takes a smoke break while his friend George snaps this picture. Both riders were fond of taking trips through Thurmont, Maryland, located outside of Frederick. The machines are both tagged with 1922 Maryland plates. Remember when smoking and motorcycle riding were both safe?

The 1931 Models Are Out

Better equipped, better looking, and better performing than ever. Twins, Single, and Sidecars — wide price range. Model shown is the new "45" Twin.

GREATEST SPORT ON WHEELS

TWIST the throttle of your Harley-Davidson, and the road is yours. Flashing speed and thrilling power answer your every whim. Was that a hill you just zoomed over? Did that fellow in the new Eight think he had something under the hood?

Let more sluggish souls have their sedans. You want the ever-new thrills of motorcycling—a spirited mount to ride — an eager Harley-Davidson that is both a pal and a trusted servant. You want the "Greatest Sport on Wheels" — and it costs *so little!*

See the new models. A nearby Harley-Davidson Dealer has them—and an easy Pay-As-You-Ride Plan that will interest you.

Mail the Coupon for illustrated literature.

Ride a **HARLEY-DAVIDSON** **Mail Coupon**

HARLEY-DAVIDSON MOTOR COMPANY, Dept. P., Milwaukee, Wis.
Interested in your motorcycles. Send literature.
Name..
Address...
My age is ☐ 16-19 years, ☐ 20-30 years, ☐ 31 years and up, ☐ under 16 years. Check your age group.

Dressed this way, these two women wouldn't get far. This bike is a 1912 model 8A single-cylinder Harley-Davidson. It required vigorous pedaling to start the 35-cubic-inch engine, something not easily done with a dress on! This bike is a belt-drive model with an adjustable idler pulley to engage the drive to the rear wheel. The rear hub unit was manufactured by Aurora Machinery Company, the same people who made engines for Indian, and later marketed their own Thor brand motorcycles. According to Motor Company records, 9,571 machines were made in 1912. The bike is equipped with a gas headlamp for night riding, and has a trusty tire pump mounted off the left side of the forks.

Far from the Beaten Track

Be independent of train service. Blaze new trails. Let fancy guide you over the lanes and side roads, far from the beaten track.

Out there you will find the real springtime that is yours and your pal's as you skim along on your

Harley-Davidson

Just as it was the mount of the Yanks and Allies, so it is the mount of every red-blooded outdoor man who appreciates readiness to go anywhere, any time.

Let your dealer show you the motorcycle that is being talked about.

Harley-Davidson Motor Co.
Milwaukee, Wis.

Please Mention Popular Mechanics

Bob Tyson

From the beginning, Harley-Davidson established its reputation by building dependable machines, and reliability was a strong selling point for early motorcyclists. Its equally impressive dealer network carried a lot of weight with cyclists, giving many the confidence to take long trips without worry of breaking down. In this photo, a 1925 seventy-four-cubic-inch twin model JD with sidecar, takes a carefree trip from Baltimore, Maryland, to Philadelphia, Pennsylvania, a distance of about one hundred miles. Harley-Davidson claimed this machine was capable of 40 to 60 miles per gallon, making it an excellent choice for sidecar duty. Spacer plates about one-eighth-inch thick were installed on J models intended for sidecar use to lower the compression slightly, allowing the engine to run cooler than the high compression version.

MOTORCYCLING

The Greatest Sport of them ALL!

3
Polo Anyone?

One thing that can be said about motorcyclists is that they are a daring group of people. Just to climb aboard one of these machines requires a greater-than-average thrill seeker. This was especially true in the early days of motorcycling, when it was still a new mode of transportation. After a while though, there was always someone looking for something new to do with his machine. At first it may have been satisfying enough to just ride down the road while maintaining balance and waving to a neighbor, but just like today, folks became bored quickly and were always on the lookout for that next new thing. Just as the bicycling craze had quite naturally evolved into a sport of racing and competition, it only seemed right that motorcycles should compete as well.

The sheer diversity of motorcycle competition was quite amazing. There were hill climbs and enduros, ice racing and stunt riding. This thing called motorcycling, this "sport of sports," seemed to have no boundaries. Riders were eager to test their skills doing any number of crazy things with their machines.

Manufacturers were glad to see their machines used for racing events and the like, because among the motorcycling crowds, word of good machines traveled fast, and that meant increased sales for the companies. Machines that couldn't take the punishment were quickly dismissed by the motoring public, and usually died a silent death. Many manufacturers never produced more than a few machines, owing to the poor quality of their product. The companies that did survive, even briefly, learned valuable product development lessons from watching competitors go out of business. Just as early aviators began to push the limits of their aircraft, so did their counterparts on two-wheeled machines. Barnstorming was not limited to airplanes. Motorcyclists began to cultivate quite an image for themselves as daredevils, too.

Hill Climbing

Hill climbing was one of the first events to surface as motorcycles grew in popularity. At first, it wasn't much more than a few fellows boasting about whose machine could make it up the hill beside the stream. Bone stock bikes were run up the hill until they just didn't have any more power to go farther. Then, little by little, owners removed fenders and other unnecessary parts such as headlights, toolboxes, and rear stands, to lighten the machines.

People would actually gather to watch these machines run up the hills, perhaps hoping for a spectacular spill here and there. The hills began to get steeper, eventually as steep as a 75 percent grade, and over time, motorcycles became faster and more highly modified for the sole purpose of hill climbing. Some of the better riders during the peak of hill climbing popularity achieved almost legendary status within the motorcycling community. A few were lucky enough to be paid by the factory of the particular brand that they rode. Traveling around the country from meet to meet, trying to make each ride your best, was definitely a tough way to earn a

View from the other side of the hill at a local Maryland hill climb in the 1920s. Perhaps this was still early in the meet, and could be a practice run. As hill climbing gained popularity in the mid to late 1920s, thousands of spectators would attend meets. Some of the riders were very well known in the motorcycling community, and attracted many fans to watch them ride. Some of the better-known riders were Howard Mitzel, Orrie Steel, and Gene Rhyne, all of whom rode Indians. Joe Petrali, who was also very well known, rode Super X machines before switching to Harley-Davidson.

living. Hill climbing enjoyed its greatest period of popularity from the mid-1920s through the early 1930s, drawing crowds of ten thousand spectators and more. After paying a small fee for admission, perhaps in the neighborhood of 25 cents, fans proceeded to the area of the hill, and found someplace comfortable to sit back and watch the thrills and spills. There were many spills to see, as one by one, the riders tried to coax their machines up a 300-foot-high hill. An electric timing device was used to score the rider's elapsed time to within one tenth of a second, so there would be no doubt as to who had the quickest time up the hill. The machines were split up into classes based on the engine size, usually either 45-cubic-inch or 74-cubic-inch categories.

All of the contestants at an "official" hill climb were required to be members of the American Motorcycle Association in order to compete. Women were not allowed to ride at hill climb events. They could attend only as spectators. Maybe that's why we don't see any women riders today! Some of the better-known hill climb riders on Harley-Davidsons were names like Joe Petrali, "Kid" Fischer, Dudley Perkins, Herb Reiber, Don Smith, and Windy Lindstrom. Hailing from the California area, Lindstrom actually won more than three hundred hill climbs between 1925 and 1930. Joe Petrali also made quite a name for himself, by competing in hill climbs, flat track races, and record-breaking land-speed runs at Daytona Beach.

Speedway Racing

While some motorcyclists were making mountain goats out of their machines, others were tearing up the speedway tracks. There were board tracks, which were long, banked motordromes made with wood planks laid end to end, cinder tracks, dirt tracks, and more. From the earliest bikes onward, racing had played an important part in development of the machinery, and the race-

Fast action on a cinder track. Riders wore steel plates on their left shoe to help keep the machines upright while crossing them up in the turns. The steel plate idea is credited to rider Maldwyn Jones, believed to be the first to use the plate. Jones was a factory rider for Merkel, but changed to Harley-Davidson after Merkel went out of business in 1916.

track was the ultimate testing ground. Here was the place that separated the men from the boys, the great machines from the average machines.

Harley-Davidson had no interest in the racing game for the first ten years of its existence, while many of the other manufacturers were refining their products from racetrack results. The Cyclone company was one such manufacturer, lasting only four years, yet building a reputation as a force to be reckoned with on the racetrack. Harley-Davidson reluctantly found itself being drawn into the game sometime around 1913, after taking notice of their own machines winning local races. Before the Motor Company got involved in racing, they made a point of it to boast the fact that even though they didn't endorse or support racing, they were justifiably proud that Harley-Davidson motorcycles were winning races. When they finally made the decision in 1913 to begin a racing program, they went into it full throttle. They were in it to win!

Harley-Davidson put together an impressive team of engineers, technicians, and riders to staff their racing department. One tip-off that Harley-Davidson was planning to get into racing came when H-D hired an engineer responsible for racing successes at Thor Motorcycle Company. His name was Bill Ottaway, and his reputation for technical knowledge carried a lot of weight. He became head of Harley's factory racing department and remained in that position until the era of long tracks and board track racing came to an end. The short tracks, or Motordromes, reached the peak of their popularity in 1912. Some of the longer board tracks remained running into the late 1920s. During this time, William Ottaway recruited many of Harley's best riders in the racing circuit. Jim Davis, Andy Hader, and once again, Joe Petrali were among these top riders. Harley-Davidson kept a hand in racing from 1914 through 1922, before withdrawing most of their factory sponsorship and leaving things to the "privateers." Their logic was that they had established themselves as a winner in every venue of racing and did not need to prove the point anymore. The factory continued making its racing models available to racers, however, even though the support was no longer offered. Harley-Davidson renewed their competition support later in the 1920s, but racing interest declined dramatically in the early 1930s, due in part to several tragic accidents involving riders and spectators alike. Of all the different sports of motorcycle competition, only hill climbing continued to enjoy large crowds and increased press. Harley-Davidson continued to develop better and faster racing machines and managed to break some records in the process.

Not until 1934 did motorcycle racing gain renewed interest with the introduction of Class C racing. The main purpose behind this class was to allow amateurs to compete without the support of the factories, which gave everyone a more equal chance. The machines were limited to 45-cubic-inch displacement, and had to have side valve configuration. The bikes were also required to be owned by the men who rode them. Because of the engine displacement and configuration specified, it was clear that Indian and Harley-Davidson would be the main stars of this class.

Enduro Meets

Another form of racing popular in the early days was the field enduro meet, which attracted all kinds of motorcycle enthusiasts with their mostly stock machines. Riders might remove some of the accessories from their bikes to compete in these events, but most of the bikes were ridden into the meet in street form. These meets were held in a variety of terrain and conditions, and the contestants were timed over a set course with obstacles to avoid or cross, and sometimes even a stream to ford. One of the best-known enduros of this type was the Jack Pine Enduro, held in rural Michigan. Named for the abundance of pine trees in the area, this meet was sponsored by the Lansing Motorcycle Club and became known for its coveted trophy of a cowbell engraved with the win-

Riders gather at a field enduro in the late 1920s. These events encouraged riders to bring their machines out for a little fun. The bikes were fully equipped road machines, and not set up for off road riding, so many took some hard knocks on these enduros. Riders were timed over a pre-determined course, over a variety of terrain. It looks like several different brands of machines lined up waiting to start.

ner's name. First begun in 1923, the winner of the Jack Pine that year was a rider named Oscar Lenz. A man by the name of A. Pond took the prize in 1924, but Lenz went on to win first place again in 1925, 1926, and 1927. Dan Raymond took home the cowbell in 1928 and 1929, but William H. Davidson, son of H-D founder William A. Davidson, competed in and won the 1930 Jack Pine, much to the delight of the Motor Company. Davidson took great pride in his riding skills and later went on to become president of the Harley-Davidson Motor Company. Oscar Lenz managed to take the win again in 1932, tying for first place with rival Dan Raymond. Lenz was declared co-champion with Raymond for 1932. According to Motor Company records, this 1932 run marked the eighth consecutive year that Harley-Davidson machines had won this event. Thirty-nine entrants started the 515-mile course, but only 21 finished. It was quite an accomplishment to muscle a big bike through such a long course!

Polo, of Course!

Of all the ways to use motorcycles in competition, none can be stranger than a polo game using motorcycles instead of horses. This "sport" is said to have started in England sometime in the 1920s. Better they should take the blame for such craziness than us Yanks! As its name suggests, thrills and spills were common, and man and machine alike came out much worse for wear after a good game. In the United States, leagues were formed in the mid-1920s, and games were played under AMA rules. Each team was allowed to have five

No, it's not some college stunt, it really is a polo game on motorcycles! This photo was taken in the early 1920s somewhere in the northeast section of the country, and teams regularly played in front of spectators. As you might imagine, injuries were common, especially when the bikes collided at 30 or 40 miles per hour. The game was played as if the riders were on horses, only a little faster!

men on the field, including a goalie, all mounted on their stripped-down machines. The field size was set at 300 feet long, and 200 wide, with a 20-foot-wide goal at each end. A normal soccer ball was kicked toward the opposing goal, and the goalie was empowered to use any method necessary to block the goal. There were penalties for unnecessary roughness, though it's hard to imagine how referees might make the call! Makes you want to cry, thinking of all those J models crashing into each other, doesn't it?

The Need for Speed

During the ups and downs of all the board track racing, enduros, and hill climbs, manufacturers gathered lots of valuable information for improvements and refinements to their machines. Even when Harley-Davidson wasn't active in the racing game, they saw what worked and what didn't, and used that knowledge in building better bikes. As a racer, rider Joe Petrali was one source of feedback to the Motor Company. Even though he was known to switch back and forth between Super X and Harley-Davidson, Petrali provided

Motorcycle fans get a close-up look at the 1936 Harley-Davidson Knucklehead that legendary rider Joe Petrali rode to a new American record of 136.183 miles per hour. This record breaking run was made in Daytona, Florida in March of 1937. The machine is a 61 cubic inch overhead valve twin, with magneto ignition. The bike was run without its streamlined tail section, due to poor handling with the tail in place. The fairing over the front end was actually fabricated from a gas tank. Photo taken in Daytona, just days after Petrali's run.

tips and suggestions to H-D chief of engineering Bill Harley during the peak of his racing days. He then culminated a brilliant racing career by piloting a 1937 sixty-one-cubic-inch overhead valve to a record speed of 136.183 m.p.h. on the sands of Daytona Beach, in March of that year. The special streamlined machine suffered handling problems at high speed, and had to be driven without its body work for the record-breaking run. This same bike is now on display at the York factory museum.

Anyone who doubts how much power these early machines made need only look at this image to change his mind. Overhead valve motors were quite capable of reaching 7,000 r.p.m., and the tremendous gear ratios enabled the machines to bring up the front wheel if the rider couldn't stay over the top of the bars.

A break in speedway racing at Reading, Pennsylvania, raceway in 1935. Although the rider's and tuner's names are not known, these Class A speedway machines were thrilling to watch. The machine in the foreground is equipped with JAP front forks, a popular racing conversion. The J.A. Prestwich company manufactured complete motorcycles for a brief period, then later made engines and chassis parts, such as this type of front fork for speedway racing use. Typically, these machines ran on a quarter-mile dirt track, and were limited to 500 cc engine displacement. The bikes ran on alcohol fuel, and developed close to 40 horsepower in a 230-pound package. It was in this racing venue that H-D rider Joe Petrali won every Class A national championship race in 1935, while simultaneously holding top honors for 45-cubic-inch hill climbing.

In this view of the field meet, riders are attempting to start their machines, giving one the idea that they were using the "Monte Carlo" start. At least one four-cylinder is visible, but most machines are Harley or Indian V-twins. By the late 1920s, only a few choices remained to riders who preferred something other than H-D.

An Indian Chief leads the way past a checkpoint on the enduro, followed closely by an unidentified machine. Safety equipment? What safety equipment? Most riders took their chances riding without helmets or eye protection, although goggles were a popular item for motorcyclists. Most machines were completely stock, with full fenders, lights, and the like. Maybe that's why it's so hard to find an old machine with all the small parts intact!

Jack Pine Run...Won by Harley-Davidson
8th CONSECUTIVE TIME

Don Raymond, American Road Champion for 1932, also winner the bells and the famous Cow Bell Trophy for 1932.

The Cow Bell Trophy, emblem of the National Jack Pine Run and carried by the winner in the preceding year's run to each Jack Pine Trial.

Oscar C. Lenz, who tied with Don Raymond for first place in the 1932 Jack Pine Run and was declared co-champion.

Raymond and Lenz, on Harley-Davidsons, Tie for First Place with a High Score of 994 Points Each

Lansing, Mich., Sept. 6th — Don Raymond, winner of the 1931 Jack Pine Run and Oscar Lenz, champion of former years, tied for first place in the 1932 Run, which was the 10th annual repetition of this famous endurance classic. Both riders, scoring 994 points each out of a possible 1000 points, rode Harley-Davidsons. Raymond piloting a 74 Big Twin and Lenz riding a 45 Twin. This victory on the part of these two famous riders, makes it the 8th consecutive year that Harley-Davidson riders have captured first place in this national competition.

Not only did Harley-Davidson capture the honors in the Class A solo competition but the world renowned Harley-Davidson horse-power, stamina and reliability was responsible for victory in all other classes of competition but one. In the Class A Sidecar event, Oswald Lenz repeated his victory of a year ago with a score of 933 points, finishing 236 points ahead of his next nearest competitor in this event.

In the Class B Sidecar, Frank Hennen of New York, riding a Harley-Davidson, finished first and in the Club Team Class the Grand Rapids, Michigan Club with McGovern, Thompson and Nichols, all on Harley-Davidson, captured the laurels. The factory team prize was carried away by Oscar Lenz, Joe Ryan and Herman Voichick, all Harley-Davidson riders, also.

Most Difficult of all Runs • • • This year, The National Jack Pine Run was laid out to be the most gruelling of all in the history of this famous endurance trial. Only 21 out of 39 entrants finished the difficult 515-mile course and 16 of those were Harley-Davidson riders. This, in itself, in addition to the victories, is a remarkable tribute to Harley-Davidson ruggedness and reliability.

Co-Champion Ruling by Officials

Because Raymond and Lenz rode motorcycles of different classifications, the officials decided upon a co-championship ruling. Raymond will retain the cow bell and receives the Lansing State Journal permanent silver trophy. Lenz will receive a duplicate silver trophy from the American Motorcycle Association and will wear the cow bell on the second day in next year's run. The Lansing Motorcycle Club and the State Journal, who promoted the trial jointly, were hosts to the riders at the start and finish of the run.

In this National Championship Endurance Trial, Harley-Davidson again demonstrated its all-around superiority over all other motorcycles. When you ride a Harley-Davidson you Ride a Winner!

HARLEY-DAVIDSON MOTOR CO.
MILWAUKEE   WISCONSIN

SUMMARIES:

Class A Solo

	Points
1. Don Raymond, Harley-Davidson	994*
2. Oscar C. Lenz, Harley-Davidson	994*
3. Lewis Kensington, Harley-Davidson	992
4. G. C. McGowan, Harley-Davidson	921
5. George Hall	898

Class A Sidecar

	Points
1. Oswald Lenz, Harley-Davidson	933
2. Red Ratledge, Harley-Davidson	660
3. Wm. Shortwave	655
4. Dan Biron, Harley-Davidson	550

Class B Solo

	Points
1. Al Waithrine	357
2. Ray La Grow	293
3. Milton Goldbert, Harley-Davidson	194

Club Team Class

	Points
1. Grand Rapids M. C.	Harley-Davidson
2. Saginaw M. C.	
3. Lansing M. C.	Harley-Davidson
4. Flower M. C.	Harley-Davidson

Factory Team Class

1. Harley-Davidson	Oscar Lenz, Joe Ryan, Herman Voichick

Class A Sidecar (continued)

	Miles
5. Lee Iturbiler, Harley-Davidson	859
6. Jack Thompson, Harley-Davidson	788
7. Earl Robinson, Harley-Davidson	765
8. A. Snadded, Harley-Davidson	660
9. Al Quarles	442

We See four points

	Miles
1. Vic Rauh, Harley-Davidson	893
2. W. A. Goodrich, Harley-Davidson	855
3. Wm. Connelly, Harley-Davidson	650
4. Jack Robie, Harley-Davidson	276
5. Joe Ryan, Harley-Davidson	260
6. Lee C. Smith	200

Class B Sidecar

1. Frank Hennen, Harley-Davidson	
2. E. T. Myers, Harley-Davidson	
3. Freeman Scott, Harley-Davidson	.085

RIDE A WINNER!

HARLEY-DAVIDSON WINS NATIONAL CHAMPIONSHIP HILLCLIMB
(EASTERN DIVISION)

3 of the 5 Events at Rochester, N. Y. Go to Harley-Davidson Riders

ROCHESTER, N. Y., Sept. 13—Three Harley-Davidson mounted hillclimbing champions emerged from the clouds of dust which hung over Egypt Hill near here today as 52 of the country's best riders battled for supremacy—Russell (Kid) Fischer of Milwaukee, Wis., Oke Hedman of Worcester, Mass., and Don Smith of Dennison, Tex. By their combined efforts Harley-Davidson took 3 of the 5 events to win the season's premier hillclimb by a comfortable margin.

In the opener, the 21 cu. in. Expert event, Don Smith caught the fancy of the crowd by putting his Harley-Davidson Single over the top in 15.14 seconds. He was the only rider who got over in this event. Hedman then copped the 45 cu. in. Amateur, with Oliver Clow of Fresno, Calif., a Harley-Davidson rider, in second place.

By the time the 61 cu. in. Professional event was called the hill was so rough that no one could top it. Kid Fischer took one look at the rutted, humpy incline, clenched his teeth more firmly in his stogie and plowed up to the 320-ft. mark for first place. Windy Lindstrom, Pacific Coast Champion in 1930 and high point winner on the Coast this season, made a whirlwind attempt to beat the Kid, but dug in one foot short of Fischer's mark.

RUSSELL (KID) FISCHER
61 Professional Champion

The picture above shows Fischer and the Harley-Davidson which carried him to victory in the 61 cu. in. Professional event. Note the cigar tucked in the corner of his face, without which he readily admits he can't climb hills. This is Fischer's first year as a professional rider. After his victorious ride at Rochester he wonders why he didn't turn pro long ago.

Harley-Davidson Wins Most Points

In the point competition that preceded the big event Harley-Davidson won more points than any other make. Herb Reiber and Windy Lindstrom, the two famous Harley-Davidson pros, outclassed the entire field. Each won more points and more first places in point hillclimbs than any other pro riders in the country. In the professional class, Harley-Davidson won more points than all other makes combined.

And in the amateur ranks, Hedman, Jenkins and Clow each won high point honors in their divisions. Clow and Hedman together accounted for 14 first places out of a possible 20 in the 45 Amateur events. Harley-Davidson riders headed the official A. M. A. point standings in 6 of the 7 divisions.

HARLEY-DAVIDSON MOTOR CO • MILWAUKEE, WIS.

RIDE A WINNER!

COMPLETE RESULTS

21.35 cu. in. Expert

1st	Don Smith	Harley-Davidson	15-14/100 sec.
2nd	Reggie Pink		290 feet
3rd	O. W. Cassedy	Harley-Davidson	270 feet
4th	J. W. Hill		268 feet
5th	A. Jenkins	Harley-Davidson	267 feet

45 cu. in Professional

1st	Gene Rhyne		14-35, 100 sec.
2nd	Ralph Moore	Harley-Davidson	15-88, 100 sec.
3rd	Reggie Pink		79-83, 100 sec.*
4th	S. McClintock	Harley-Davidson	19-85, 100 sec.*
5th	L. McKinney		20- 4 100 sec.

*Pink won run-off for tie.

45 cu. in. Amateur

1st	Oke Hedman	Harley-Davidson	16--95, 100 sec.
2nd	Oliver Clow	Harley-Davidson	321 feet
3rd	S. Potarek		310 feet
4th	Wm. Alveson		300 feet
5th	W. Caernaigag		296 feet

61 cu. in. Professional

1st	Russell Fischer	Harley-Davidson	320 feet
2nd	Windy Lindstrom	Harley-Davidson	319 feet
3rd	L. McKinney		315 feet
4th	Reggie Pink		312 feet
5th	Gene Rhyne		304 feet

80 cu. in. Amateur

1st	S. Potarek		327 feet
2nd	P. Gebobacker		251 feet
3rd	J. Gebobacker		229 feet*
4th	J. Jozumt		229 feet*
5th	J. Sypek	Harley-Davidson	229 feet

*Gebobacker won run-off for tie.

OKE HEDMAN
45 Amateur Champion

Oke hails from Worcester, Mass. and has been doing his stuff on Harley-Davidsons for several years. This year he broke into the spotlight by winning high point honors in the 45 Amateur division as well as copping this event at Rochester.

DON SMITH
21 Expert Champion

History repeats! For the second consecutive year, Don Smith, Dennison, Texas, entered the 21 event of a National Championship Hill-climb. Smith was the only rider over the top in this event at Muskogee in 1938 as well as at Rochester this year.

HARLEY~DAVIDSON

Hill climbing started out this way, by regular guys riding their own street machines up the local dirt mound. Often the bikes were stripped of unessential parts like lights, fenders, and mufflers. At such gatherings, the only timing device to measure the results would be the watch owned by an observer. Motorcycle clubs began to organize and advertise these events, and in a relatively short period of time, hill climbing became one of the most popular motorcycle sports in the country. This photograph was taken around 1919.

Hill climbing action here! It looks as though the rider is having difficulty staying on the machine. His right leg is beginning to come back, and up away from the floor-board. Machines like this one were capable of about 30 to 40 miles per hour uphill, fast enough to get hurt without safety equipment.

GLIDER of the HIGHWAY!

SOARING down the roads — effortless — silent — smooth — the Harley-Davidson is a true Glider of the Highway. It responds instantly to every whim — answers every sway of your body.

Give the throttle a twist and instantly your Twin becomes a brute of a thing — pulsing with power — eager to snort over hills, or race down a straightaway. That's motorcycling — sport of a thousand thrills!

So inexpensive, too. A Harley-Davidson costs little to buy — almost nothing to run.

Let your Dealer show you the 1931 Twins, Single, and Sidecars. Ask about his Pay-As-You-Ride Plan.

Mail Coupon for Literature

Ride a **HARLEY-DAVIDSON**

HARLEY-DAVIDSON MOTOR COMPANY
Dept. P., Milwaukee, Wis.
Interested in your motorcycles. Send literature.
Name..
Address..
My age is ( ) 16-19 years, ( ) 20-30 years, ( ) 31 years and up, ( ) under 16 years.
Check your age group.

87

Rider Freddie Marsh charges up the hill at a Meriden, Connecticut, meet in the fall of 1931. Heavy chains on the rear tire help provide extra traction in the loose stone and dirt surface of the hill. The boundary lines of the hill are marked by the twine strung along wood posts up the hill, and a rider would be disqualified if he ran out of the marked course. This sometimes made for some spectacular acrobatics by the riders, as they struggled to keep the bikes pointed in the right direction. These early hill climber motorcycles were basically stripped-down machines with stock wheel base frames, as compared with hill climbing bikes of today, with radically stretched frames. This made the task of staying on the bike more difficult on the steep hills, which forced the rider to lean as far forward as possible to keep the front wheel in contact with the dirt.

View from the top of the Enfield, Massachusetts, hill as rider Orrie Steele makes it over. Security was provided by a local police officer. He can be seen standing at the crest of the hill alongside a meet official. Riders were required to belong to the American Motorcyclist Association in order to compete at a national meet. Riders were clocked by an electric timing device, which was started when the rider's machine broke a string across the bottom of the hill. If and when the rider crossed the top of the hill, he broke a second cord, which closed a switch and stopped the timer. The device was accurate to one-tenth of a second!

A rolling advertisement for upcoming championship motorcycle races at the York, Pennsylvania, fairgrounds in 1932. The small print on the sign tells of the planned T T races, and on the following day, a hill climb, enough to satisfy the most die-hard motorcycle fans.

Spectators at a motorcycle hill climb in Meriden, Connecticut, go to new heights to see all the action. Although the ticket price of only 50 cents gave you entrance to the meet, it didn't guarantee you a good seat! The ticket stub had a twofold purpose for the enthusiast. It came with a built-in buttonhole so that it could be worn at the meet, and the back of the ticket was printed with a disclaimer for injury or accident to the spectator while on the club premises. This meet was organized by the Meriden Motorcycle Club, and was held according to the AMA rules in effect on October 5, 1931. This particular hill climb attracted its share of well-known riders, including Indian riders Orie Steele, Howard Mitzell, and king of the amateurs, "Red House." Orie Steele set the record for the day with the fastest time of 5.71 seconds. This time was the best time for any class, not just the 45-cubic-inch class that Steele rode in! Although the photographer had a preference for the Indian riders at this meet, one look at the spectators' machines shows that Harley-Davidson was well represented too.

Close inspection of this photo appears to show a single-cylinder machine right at the marker flag. Incline is greater than it appears, and the rider is bent forward, helping to keep the front end stable. Many different brands of motorcycles were used in hill climbing. Names like Super X and Indian were as widely used as Harley-Davidsons. At professional hill-climb meets, safety equipment would include some kind of helmet for the rider, and a leather strap to loop around the rider's wrist. If and when he unloaded, the strap would pull a spring clip off of the ignition, killing the engine and stopping the bike. This would not prevent the motorcycle from rolling back down the hill, or sliding to an area that was hard to reach. For this a crew of men would stay on the side of the hill, to snare any machine that lost its rider and prevent it from slipping back down the hill.

What kind of people watched hill climbs? Mostly just average people who enjoyed motorcycles, and all the things that motorcycles did. Take a close look at these spectators at this small meet. Ladies wearing dresses and hats, and men with white shirts and hats. Must have been an AMA meet! Not too many shirts and ties are seen at motorcycle meets today!

A professional hill climb in Enfield, Massachusetts, in May of 1930. As evident by the number of automobiles parked below the hill, this was a national meet. These events would draw more than 2,000 people, and riders from as far away as Los Angeles would enter the competition. Amateur champion "Red" House was a big draw at this meet. Red later turned pro, riding for the Indian Company. The tower in the left foreground is the official's vantage point and was usually situated near the top of the hill. This hill was more than 250 feet high at a 60-degree incline!

With his goggles on his helmet, the rider to the far left must have felt confident about taking the lead early in this cinder track heat race. Being in the rear of the pack meant getting peppered with cinders and dust. These overhead valve singles were the basis for Class A racing, popular into the mid-1930s, before Class C took the spotlight. Harley-Davidson's entry in this class was its model CAC, 30.50-cubic-inch racer. Though few of these little powerhouse machines were made, they left their mark on speedway racing. Speeds of more than 100 miles per hour were typical of these bikes, and engines tached up to 6,000 r.p.m. The direct-drive bikes had to be pushed to start, and ran on alcohol-based fuel. The machines carried a small oil tank under the seat for oiling the rear chain.

An unidentified rider poses in the pits during a Class "C" racing event. He is astride a WR model Harley-Davidson racer. This factory-built racing machine was a 45-cubic-inch flathead machine equipped with a three-speed transmission. This bike appears to have battery ignition, but many were supplied with a magneto with only a kill switch. Extra wheels and tires are visible behind the bike.

It looks as if Harley's main competition has shown up today! This Indian Chief is ready to run in a Class "C" event, but not before the rider's family poses for a group photo. Judging from the automobiles behind them, this photo was taken in the late 1930s. Many riders were privateers, financing their machines with their own money, and often not winning anything, just racing for the sake of having fun.

Riders ready their machines in the pits before the main event of a Class "C" race. The Indian is believed to be the same machine seen in the foregoing photo, although the number plate seems to have been removed.

The *Only Cure* for our deplorable traffic conditions!

4

The Good Old Days

How often have you heard someone talk about "the good old days"? Did they reminisce as if they would rather be back in that time? Did you ever wonder what it must have been like, being a motorcyclist in the early days? What if you could transport yourself back to the turn of the century, and find out firsthand whether the "good old days" really were that good. To be sure, America was a very exciting place to be when the twentieth century came rolling in. The growing nation was just beginning to flex its industrial muscles, and change was in the air.

Imagine yourself whisked back through time to the year 1910. You find yourself standing on a busy street corner in downtown Baltimore City. The streets are filled with men and women going about their business, working, shopping, or just plain socializing. Horse-drawn carriages and automobiles alike randomly make their way up and down both sides of the street. Bicycles seem to be everywhere, dodging the autos as they move along. You notice that most of the men you see are wearing hats, and many are also dressed in coat and tie, while the ladies all appear to be dressed

A well-dressed father and son proudly pose with their bicycles in front of their South Baltimore row home. In the spring of 1910, they no doubt believed, as did hundreds of thousands of other Americans, that bicycles were still the cheapest and best way to get around. As Henry Ford's mass-produced cars began to roll off the assembly line, that way of thinking would change forever. Ford's economical, yet practical automobiles probably changed the minds of many would-be motorcycle owners as well. This was one of the main reasons motorcycles became a recreational vehicle in the early years. Automobiles were sometimes cheaper to buy than motorcycles, due in part to the larger number of cars being built, and because, during this era, many operations of motorcycle manufacturing were still done by hand.

up for their outing in the city. A motorcycle and sidecar rig come chugging down the street behind a "Tin Lizzie" Model T, the male rider and his female companion in the sidecar both wearing goggles. Motorcycles were beginning to become a common sight, with motorcycle registrations numbering about 86,000 in 1910, and already there were financial institutions willing to lend money for the purchase of a new machine. Not really much different from the cities of today, you think, except maybe the people were generally better dressed.

In transportation, however, things were a lot different from just ten years earlier. Had you transported back to the same place but to the year 1900, you would have seen quite a different sight. Horses and carriages would be the rule, with perhaps only an occasional automobile. In the year 1900, there were only about 8,000 automobiles in the entire nation. They were still considered something of a novelty. Most people were content to stick with the proven bicycle, rather than attempt to operate a gasoline-powered vehicle. Who in his right mind would want to be seen driving such a contraption? By 1912, however, there would be more than a million people willing to be seen in an automobile.

Wheels and Things

Sometime around 1885, an Englishman named J. K. Starley produced what is believed to have been the first commercially successful safety bicycle. This bicycle had wheels of equal size (unlike its cousin, the older penny-farthing), and was propelled by a chain-and-sprocket system. It had solid tires and rode a little on the rough side, yet it was a vast improvement over the high-wheeled penny-farthing of the 1870s. When Irish veterinarian John Dunlop perfected the pneumatic tire in 1889, life got a whole lot easier for bicyclists. The two-wheeled vehicle was now comfortable and smooth riding, making it more appealing to the masses. Dozens

At the end of the nineteenth century, bicycle racing was big business, and the racers themselves were as popular as Major League baseball players are today. Fans followed the racing circuit year round, even if it sometimes meant riding the trains two or three hundred miles just to see a race. The man astride the bike is Jack White, a popular bicycle racing champion in Maryland during the late 1800s. Like the teams of Bill Harley and Arthur Davidson, and George Hendee and Oscar Hedstrom, he too knew that bicycles were destined to go much faster. After becoming friends with another local tinker named Richard Schaffer, they joined forces to create their version of the powered motorbike. Unfortunately for them, they chose steam power over gasoline, and the rest, as they say, is history.

of cycle manufacturers sold their products to Americans eager to try the latest transportation device. By the end of the 1800s, it was estimated that there were more than four million bicycles in use in the United States. All types of manufacturing companies got into the bicycle business. Firearm companies, sewing machine manufacturers, carriage builders, and others were quick to get hold of a piece of the market. An organization to promote the interests of bicyclists in America was formed called the League of American Wheelmen. They exerted enough influence with the federal government to campaign for better and more numerous roads in the cities. There were publications dedicated solely to bicycling, and as early as 1894, the soon-to-be-famous map maker, Rand-McNally, had published a bicycle road map. During this national craze with the bicycle, another event was unfolding that would forever alter the course of the young nation.

Birth of the Automobile

The gasoline engine was beginning to show promise as a power source for vehicles of all types. By the 1890s, people such as Frank Duryea and Henry Ford were experimenting with carriages fitted with small internal combustion engines. Duryea is said to have driven the first successful automobile in 1893, while Henry Ford road tested his "auto" in the year 1896. Other builders would soon follow these two automotive pioneers. Most Americans put little faith in these early machines, and continued to rely on their bicycles and horses. There were, however, a handful of people in

The steam-powered creation of former bicycle racer Jack White and inventor Richard Schaffer was the feature story of a 1950 Baltimore newspaper, fifty-two years after it was built. According to the accompanying text related by the aging Jack White, the steam-powered cycle could hit speeds of over 50 miles per hour, without making a sound. The cycle was banned from operating in a local Baltimore city park because it frightened horses, which were the more common mode of transportation at that time. The inventors remarked that they chose steam power for their bike because the gasoline engines of 1898 were "faltering, untrustworthy contraptions." Mr. White recounted in the article that he was very sorry for disposing of the machine sometime in the 1930s, because it was cluttering up the garage. What a great piece that could have been for the Heritage Museum!

America who thought that bicycles would be a more suitable candidate for an engine than a carriage. Across the country, tinkers, mechanics, and backyard engineers were all trying to find a way to take the work out of riding a "wheel," as bicycles were often called, by adding some gasoline-assisted propulsion. This was at a time when many engineers and mechanics still believed that steam power was, and always would be, superior to gasoline engines.

Many early attempts at gasoline-powered motorbikes proved to be unreliable and inconsistent, thereby causing some designers to advocate steam power. In 1898, Baltimore residents Jack White, a former champion bicycle racer, and his close friend, Richard Shaffer, built a steam-powered motorcycle that they named the Steam Whirlwind. This machine was capable of attaining speeds of over 50 miles per hour, but required both men to be astride the machine at the same time. The man in the front of the motorcycle steered and braked, while the man on the rear operated the throttle and monitored the water level in the boiler. Despite the fact that the builders were banned from operating it in Druid Hill Park because

Howard Street in downtown Baltimore around 1910. A bicyclist casually crosses the wide street, while automobiles park on both sides. This scene is typical of a city street in 1910, with only a few cars here and there. According to motor vehicle registration records, there were already 86,000 motorcycles registered in 1910. As motor vehicles became increasingly more common in the coming years, traffic control became a serious problem. The first stop sign was erected in Detroit sometime in 1912, and two years later, in Cleveland, the very first red, yellow, and green traffic light was installed.

it scared horses, the machine was successfully operated in and around Baltimore for several years, until it became apparent that gasoline engines were getting better and steam was on its way out.

The rapid advances in gasoline engines got a lot of folks interested in the motorcycle business early on, although, contrary to popular belief, motorcycles did not just suddenly appear overnight. There was a substantial amount of trial and error in building a machine that worked, and the intense competition between the builders actually helped product development. That is, it helped to weed out the machines that weren't very good, while boosting the reputations of the ones that were better. The idea for these vehicles belonged not to the United States, unlike so many key inventions, but rather to Europe. German engineer Gottlieb Daimler is credited as the father of the modern gasoline-powered motorcycle, having developed a working model to test his small engine in 1885. Other European engineers were working on similar ideas about the same time, and it didn't take long for their American counterparts to catch up.

In the beginning, a motorcycle was looked at as a logical progression up from the bicycle. After all, most Americans had already been riding bicycles for at least a few years, and who wanted to pedal when you could just sit back and steer. Just as the bicycle was basic, real transportation for millions of Americans, so were the first motorcycles to be offered to the public. As the early makes of motorcycles became available, not only were they an affordable alternative to automobiles, but in some cases, they were priced about the same as a top-of-the-line bicycle. In 1898, the Pope Manufacturing Company, founded by Colonel Albert Pope of Boston, advertised a "chainless" shaft-drive bicycle for the price of $125. Yet just five years later in 1902, the three-horsepower Marsh Motor Cycle was unveiled for the very same price of $125. Pope eventually entered the motorcycle market in 1911, but poor management ended the company's production in 1918.

Birth of a Legend or Two

Elsewhere in the country, other individuals and partnerships developed ideas as the motorcycle began to take shape in America. It appeared that there was a market for this exciting new mode of transportation. In Springfield, Massachusetts, a young bicycle-racing champion by the name of George Hendee was interested in obtaining a motor-driven bicycle for the purpose of using it as a windbreaker for distance record attempts by cyclists. His search for a bicycle of this type led him to New York, where an inventor named Oscar Hedstrom had built such a machine. Hendee was so impressed with the design and function of Hedstrom's pacer that he propositioned the inventor to bring his work to Springfield and join forces to market this new machine. Within four months of that meeting, Hedstrom rode his new prototype over a 40-mile route from Connecticut to Springfield, Massachusetts. Thus, the humble beginnings of the Indian Motorcycle came about as these two men brought their visions of the future to life.

As Bill Harley and the Davidson brothers continued with their business venture in Milwaukee, their success went beyond their

The rider's name is Frank Krieger and the year is 1935. Like many other motorcycle enthusiasts, Krieger is ready to embark on a cross-country trip, as the writing on his saddlebags notes. He planned to leave New York City and head for California, and make a visit to the Grand Canyon on the way. His 1935 Model VL, with its 74-cubic-inch side valve engine could cruise at 60 m.p.h., while delivering over 50 miles to the gallon of gas. This machine sold for about $360 in 1935, up slightly from the low prices Harley set in the tough Depression years. Harley-Davidson knew the importance of a strong and well-represented dealer network early in their existence. Riders such as Frank Kreiger had peace of mind knowing that the extensive network of Harley dealerships could provide parts and service on cross-country journeys or local touring trips.

expectations. Plant size grew every year, and by 1912, manufacturing space occupied more than 200,000 square feet. When they filed for incorporation papers in 1907, motorcycle production was about 150 machines, but in 1912, almost 10,000 bikes left the factory. The operations at Harley-Davidson Motor Company provided employment for hundreds and hundreds of local residents, while causing many related industries to grow at the same time. Tire manufacturers, steel suppliers, and foundries all enjoyed the results of Harley-Davidson's success. It is doubtful that the four founders of Harley-Davidson Motor Company ever thought that they would become the most famous partnership in the motorcycle world.

Hard Times

It is ironic that many older folks still refer to the early twentieth century as "the good old days." Life was certainly simpler in many ways, but even hard work couldn't prevent the worst from happening. Motorcycle and automotive industries prospered through the mid-1920s, making a strong recovery after the First World War. Harley-Davidson had supplied almost 15,000 olive drab machines for Uncle Sam, and civilian sales had suffered slightly during the war. After the signing of the Armistice in November 1918, the motorcycling public was once again satisfied with the abundance of machines available. Indian bought the remains of the Ace Motorcycle Company in 1927, and marketed an Indian Ace four-cylinder machine the following year. In 1928, Harley-Davidson considered buying the Cleveland Motorcycle Manufacturing Company, which made lightweight singles and large four-cylinder machines, possibly to compete with the Indian four-cylinder machines. Cleveland was in financial trouble, and had offered to sell out to the Milwaukee firm. H-D officers finally decided not to take the chance with Cleveland, reasoning that they planned on developing their own four-cylinder motorcycle in the coming years. This proved to be a well-timed decision. In October 1929, the Wall Street Stock Market collapsed, leaving many of the smaller motorcycle companies no choice but to close their doors forever. As the Great Depression wore on into 1933, more than 15 million Americans were without work, and motorcycles were way down on the priority list for most people. Harley-Davidson produced only 3,703 machines that year, down from almost 25,000 motorcycles in 1919. If not for the conservative efforts of H-D management, and their solicitation of police agencies for business, Harley-Davidson might have succumbed to the same fate as most of the other manufacturers. H-D relied heavily on exports to keep them alive during this time. The factory was now operating at only 10 percent of its capacity, and many employees had been laid off. H-D negotiated an agreement with a Japanese company, which allowed them to sell a complete set of blueprints for most of their line to be built in Japan. Royalties were to be paid to H-D for providing engineering services, and the income allowed Harley-Davidson to keep some employees through these tough times. Only the Indian Company remained as competition for H-D, after Excelsior closed their operations in 1931.

Ice Racing, Anyone?

Winters in Goldsboro, Pennsylvania, were extremely boring, especially in 1931, but the local boys did find ways to amuse themselves from time to time. Martin Forrer was one of those local boys, and he was anxiously waiting for the ice boat races on the Susquehanna River the coming Sunday, telling the others that they should check out the river where the races would be held. Now, these boys had seen the river frozen before, but never all the way across the almost two-mile width near Division Street. Since Martin didn't own a car and rode his Harley-Davidson motorcycle most of the year, it only seemed right that he and some friends should try out their bikes on the ice. After meeting up at Hoyt's store on February 11, they rode down to the river's edge, and tested

Harley-Davidson's advertising department often called motorcycling "the sport of sports," and many people found fun and adventure with their machines. Motorized vehicles gave many the freedom to travel longer distances for work and pleasure, as shown by these two fishermen on Solomon's Island, near Maryland's Eastern Shore. According to notes written on the original photos, these 74-cubic-inch J models were ridden over 80 miles roundtrip to catch these fish. Both bikes were equipped with electric lighting, and a speedometer lamp is visible behind the speedo on the machine on the left. The small hole below the center of the clutch cover was added in 1918 to allow the rider to oil the clutch without removing the primary cover. These machines appear to be 1921 models, but the photo dates from 1924.

the thickness of the ice in several places. After discovering that it was over 18 inches thick, everyone felt pretty confident that it was OK to ride on it. It was a very cold day, but soon there were five fellas racing up and down the frozen river on their motorcycles, and according to Martin, hitting speeds of over 60 miles per hour. No one had skid chains on their machines, and the tires were smooth due to excess wear. It must have been a sight watching these boys race across the ice, with legs dangling and feet sliding, trying to keep the bikes vertical!

Somewhere about this time, while the "ice show" was still going on, Pat Brooks, the owner of the local airfield, brought one of his planes down on the ice for a landing. He was the person

Martin Forrer, of Goldsboro, Pennsylvania, doing what came natural in the wintertime—riding his Harley single on frozen lakes and rivers! The story of his harrowing ice adventure is recounted in this chapter.

promoting the ice races coming up the following Sunday, and he already knew the ice was plenty thick. He suggested that the gang ride over to an island about two miles downriver. It seemed like a great challenge, so off they went, and when all five riders made it to the island, they lit a fire to warm up. Martin's friend Davis was ready to go farther downriver, but the rest of the boys were cold, and insisted that they head back. Martin told them to go on back, and that he and Davis would be along shortly.

Martin then suggested to Davis that the two of them do something that none of the other fellows in the area had accomplished. He reasoned that if the ice was 18 inches thick on this side of the river, then it should be at least that thick on the other side, too. He and Davis set off on a diagonal course across the river, which was almost four miles in distance. The ice was rough, but by staying in low gear, they were able to negotiate the tricky, bumpy patches of ice. Martin even remarked to Davis that they should photograph their exploits, to send to the AMA magazine, but neither rider had a camera. As they rode on, it was beginning to get dark, but the shore was approaching. Martin led by about ten yards, and Davis was slowly following his tracks. As they came to the shore, the bank was steeper than it looked, so Martin decided to go downriver a little farther, near a coal wharf which had a lower-grade bank, and a road leading to the highway. With Martin less than 50 yards from the shore, the ice suddenly gave way, and he and his motorcycle instantly disappeared from Davis's sight! Davis swerved his machine, and was able to stop without running into the same hole that Martin fell through. Davis stopped his machine and got off, carefully moving over to the hole where Martin floundered in the cold water. Martin was dressed well for a winter day, with a heavy sheepskin coat, and other heavy clothing underneath, and was unable to pull himself out of the water. Davis laid down, inched over to Martin, and gradually pulled him out, as the ice broke farther away from the hole.

After both men eased themselves away from the opening, and Martin collapsed on the ice in a shivering heap, Davis let loose with hysterical laughter. Martin begged him to stop, and asked how he could laugh about such a serious thing, since his beloved motorcycle was now at the bottom of the river, which they guessed was about 18 feet deep. As Davis carefully walked around searching for a solid place to get his machine off the river, he broke through the ice as Martin had, and found himself flailing in the cold water while Martin cracked up with laughter. Martin was frozen to the ice from his wet clothes, and could not move a muscle to help his friend. Davis managed to pull himself up, and as he did, a man shouted to them from the shore. They asked him to get a boat out through the slush ice and get them both off the river, but he was unable to get the boat out that far. He shouted to both men that he would go and get in touch with the Fire and Rescue Company of Middletown, Pennsylvania, which was eight miles away. Meanwhile, two other men who were walking the ice upriver, heard the shouting and came to help. Davis asked them how to get his machine to the shore, and they told him they would help move the motorcycle since Davis's clothing was now freezing from the dunking he took, and movement was difficult. Several attempts to free

Martin from the river ice proved futile, so they said they would return with tools after getting Davis safely to shore.

It was some time before the Fire Rescue Company arrived to where Martin was still stuck fast to the ice, and very cold by this time, and he was happy to hear the voices of the crowd that had gathered on the shore to watch the rescue. The sirens from the fire truck attracted quite a bit of attention as the men raced down to the wharf with a boat and grappling hooks. The fireman shouted to Martin and asked where the man was under the ice.

Martin answered that he was the man, but they did not want to believe him. The fire chief asked where Martin's machine was, and as he shivered out his answer about it being at the bottom of the river, the laughter erupted again. As the crowd of bystanders shouted out encouragement, the fire chief, Claude Judy, directed the rescue. Three men launched the large boat, and attempted to move near Martin using grappling hooks and rope, but could not get the boat to break the ice enough to move through it. They gave up on this method, and tossed several ropes with weights to Martin, barely missing him with one of the weighted projectiles. He was able to wrap the rope around himself, and the firemen pulled him to the boat. As Martin was loaded into the ambulance, the attendants were certain that he was hysterical from the cold, but truth was, as they lifted him up on the stretcher, the cold water in his boots came running out, and up his pant legs, causing him to convulse wildly again. They arrived at the firehouse where others were awaiting the frozen riders, and hustled both men into the shower room and began to rub cold water over their bodies. This gradually made them warmer, and soon both men were able to apply hot water. By this time, many local neighbors began to come in to the firehouse with stimulants and warm-up drinks of their own, thanks mainly to the repeal of the Eighteenth Amendment!

At Davis and Martin's urging, several of the firemen, led by Johnny Patton, of Middletown, were in the boat using grappling irons in the area where the motorcycle had broken through. After several attempts, they succeeded in hooking the front forks of the bike and pulled it into shore. The men brought the machine back to the firehouse, and Martin spent about 30 minutes draining the gas and oil from the bike and checking the rest of it over. In short order, he had the bike running with no ill effects from the two-and-a-half-hour immersion!

Davis phoned a local hill climber and racer named Chick Frank, and asked him to bring some extra riding clothes so the two men could get their bikes home, and Chick told him that he would do so, if they would come have dinner with him and his wife. This offer was too good to refuse. After the meal, they returned to the firehouse to get their machines and were greeted by reporters from the Harrisburg newspaper, who wanted to know who the hero was so that they could photograph him. Martin gave the reporters a friend's name and address, and told them that his friend didn't want any attention. He knew this might cause a little trouble for his friend, but think about all the publicity for the upcoming ice races!

Martin and Davis thanked all of the firemen and the locals who helped out, tied their still-frozen clothes in a burlap bag, and headed out for the nine-mile-ride home. Martin said his bike still had about a one-inch-thick cake of ice around the gas tank, with gasoline still on the inside part of the ice. The two men later found out that due to chemicals in the river from the Bethlehem Steel plant a few miles upriver, this side of the river had never frozen completely in the last ten years! Which was why the ice on that side had given way.

At the next gathering of local riders down at Hoyt's store, one of the older motorcyclists remarked that he didn't think it was necessary to fall through river ice just to get your name in the paper, to which Martin answered, "I'll do it again for two bottles of Crab Orchard wine!"

Even with Harley-Davidson's low price of only $290 for this 1929, 45-cubic-inch flathead, many people were hard pressed to it to justify this much money on a new motorcycle. The full impact of the Great Depression had not yet been felt, but already H-D was feeling a financial crunch. In February 1929, a federal court decided that Harley-Davidson was infringing on three patents held by the Eclipse Machine Company, which manufactured transmission parts. They were awarded $1.1 million in damages, marking the beginning of a downward turn in profits for H-D. Martin Forrer, of Goldsboro, Pennsylvania, was the proud new owner of this twin-headlight-equipped machine. The dual headlights only lasted for two model years, 29 and 30, and were inadequate for night riding. The model DL was nicknamed the "three cylinder Harley" by Indian riders due to the vertical generator sticking up in the left front of the engine. The bevel-gear-driven generator allowed the 45 to use the same frame as the 21-cubic-inch single models.

This 1922 Harley J model was equipped for family functions with its comfortable sidecar. Other accessories included a front-wheel-driven speedometer, and a mechanical Klaxon horn. The headlight and taillight on this machine were gas-operated from the horizontal tank under the handlebars. These lights were nowhere near so good as electric lights, but were better than no lights at all.

Touring the battlefields at Gettysburg in 1925, when the memories of that war were only sixty years old. The three-year-old child on the cannon barrel was almost seventy years old when I began to sort through these negatives in 1988. It's quite possible that the woman in the sidecar had personal recollections of the Civil War.

SPLIT
THE AIR
Like a Rocket!

FLASHING acceleration — from start to full speed in a few seconds — is a motorcycle thrill that only a "rocket motor" could equal.

Just ride a 1932 Harley-Davidson and feel what real pick-up is. See how it shoots you away from tangled traffic. You are down the road, safe and clear, before cars are really rolling. Then the whole countryside is yours — for swift jaunt or long tour. And motorcycling costs so little!

Look over the 1932 Harley-Davidsons at your nearest dealer's. See for yourself how little they cost — at the new reduced prices — and what a convenient Pay-As-You-Ride Plan he has.

$195—at the factory—is the low price of the Harley-Davidson Single, a new model for 1932. It's a completely equipped motorcycle, with 3-speed transmission, full electric equipment and all. Wonderful value.

Ride a
HARLEY-DAVIDSON

MAIL THIS COUPON

Harley-Davidson Motor Company
Dept. P., Milwaukee, Wis.
Interested in your motorcycles. Send Literature.

Name

Address

My age is ☐ 16-19 years, ☐ 20-30 years, ☐ 31 years and up, ☐ under 16 years.
Check your age group.

When writing to advertisers please mention Popular Mechanics

R IDE A MOTORCYCLE—because it's wonderful
sport—because it's healthful and sensible—because it saves money, saves time, saves energy.

Join the Jolly Riders in their evening spins, club runs,
and glorious vacations. Harley-Davidson enthusiasts
all, eager to welcome you into their fraternity of
sport. Nobody has a better time—and it costs so little!

See for yourself how easy it is to own a Harley-Davidson—how low its upkeep is—and how much time and
money it will save you.

Ask your nearby Harley-Davidson Dealer about his
Pay-As-You-Ride Plan—and mail
the Coupon for free literature.

Ride a
HARLEY-DAVIDSON

MAIL THIS COUPON

An Indian Bobber ready for enduro competition! Stripped of fenders and lights, the machine still retains the front crash bar and stock exhaust, not to mention the fuzzy seat cover! A Harley rests nearby, thankful it still has its lights!

A visit to this monument recognizing Union Soldiers from Minnesota had special meaning for the man in this photo. His grandfather was killed in action fighting with the Minnesota division during the Civil War.

Lady Liberty was an important destination for one group of Maryland riders, since many of the riders' parents were immigrants themselves, and passed through Ellis Island not too many years earlier. This American symbol of freedom left a lasting memory in all who saw her. This photograph was taken in 1925.

Bob Tyson

Rest areas in 1925 just weren't as nice as they are today! One fearless group found this grape arbor irresistible as a photo opportunity. With the Atlantic Ocean in the background, the New Jersey shoreline had to be cold in March, but George Hoffman is looking warm in his long coat.

A group of motorcycle enthusiasts pose for a photo outside a Pennsylvania Harley-Davidson dealership right across from the local Hudson automobile dealer. The rider at center sports a winged wheel design on his jersey and wears a wide leather kidney belt to lessen the jolts of the road.

Hard as it is to believe, this Harley-Davidson may be suffering from mechanical troubles, or these boys are just sharing a funny story. Either way, this 1935 Model VL doesn't seem to be lacking attention.

A Henderson motorcycle is a thing of beauty, even to this group of young boys at summer camp in Connecticut. One look may have been all it took to hook some of these boys on the thrills of motorcycling.

Outside this Bronx, New York, Harley-Davidson dealership in 1934, a group of riders and enthusiasts pose for the camera before leaving for a local hill climb. Motorcycle dealers like this one were a great place for riders to meet and just hang out with other folks who shared their passion. This practice is still going today with the Motor Company–sponsored "Harley Owner's Group."

This unknown little girl has all she needs for security—a helmet and goggles, her teddy bear, and a nicely equipped 35 Harley-Davidson VL with sidecar. It does look as if the spare on the back of the sidecar has been used a little! The front brake lever is located on the left side of the handlebars, not the right as they are today.

Three fellas crowd around this Ariel motorcycle, in the parking area of a hill climb. Ariel was another British brand not often seen in the United States. The gentleman in the right rear is proudly wearing his Harley-Davidson wings on his sweater; no doubt his machine is the next bike over.

A Royal Enfield motorcycle from the mid-1930s sits under a tree awaiting its owner. British machines were a rare sight in the United States, where Indian and Harley-Davidson accounted for more than 90 percent of registered machines. Dealers for these bikes were few and far between, and owners often waited weeks for replacement parts. Still, they had their loyal following, and from time to time even the big two would buy a British machine to take apart and see what the boys across the big pond were up to.

A great family shot, around the motorcycle and sidecar! Too many relatives and friends to identify here, but it seems that the motorcycles were always the center of attention. This may have been a reunion of Merchant Seamen, or perhaps Navy boys. This photo was taken around 1920 in Curtiss Creek, Maryland.

A Harley rider takes a break in the shade on his 1930 Model DL flathead. This machine still sports the dual headlights used for only two years. This bike was a 45-cubic-inch Powerplant, which was introduced in 1929 and became one of the longest manufactured engines by the Motor Company. The engine was still produced as the "G" motor for three-wheeled Servi Cars up to 1973.

FREE AS A HAWK ON WING

Soar away — wherever fancy calls you. Swoop down to that little lake you've glimpsed from the highway. Wing your swift and easy way over roads and trails to new adventures — to new cities worth seeing, and new people worth meeting.

Free as a hawk you are, when you're riding a Harley-Davidson. All roads are yours. You breeze by car parades, and flit through traffic jams. You can ride as much and as far as you like, for Harley-Davidson cost-per-mile is next to nothing!

See the 1931 Harley-Davidson models at your nearest dealer's. Ask about his Pay-As-You-Ride Plan. *Mail Coupon to us for free literature.*

Ride a HARLEY-DAVIDSON

5
Mail Order Motorcycling

What was life really like during the early years of motorcycling? How did folks get along without indoor bathrooms? Where did you buy gasoline for your motor vehicle? How could you find and purchase accessories for your machine? It's not as if you could just order it from a catalog and have it delivered to your door in 1920, or could you? I won't try to answer all these questions, but surprisingly enough, mail order shopping for motorcycle parts and supplies was available as early as 1904, not long after two of the country's biggest motorcycle manufacturers got under way. The birth of low-cost transportation for average Americans opened many doors of opportunity for enterprising supply companies and individuals. They were more than ready to quench the thirst of enthusiasts eager to buy parts and supplies.

Perhaps one of the largest and best-known of the supply companies in America was MECO, which stood for, "Motorcycle Equipment Company." MECO had warehouses conveniently located on each coast. With one location in Los Angeles, California, and the other in Hammondsport, New York, delivery across the entire nation was covered. They advertised heavily in the trade publications of the day, and claimed to be the biggest jobber and manufacturer of motorcycle supplies and accessories in the United States. The company promised its customers that the items in its catalog were only the finest that could be found, and, according to company advertising, "Not a single article listed will be found undesirable." They also stated that they tested every product in the catalog, and if it was found to be less than expected by the customer, the customer's money would be returned. It's fairly hard to find those practices in use by businesses today, so in 1904, that really was a good deal! MECO also promised to pay all transportation charges on any items ordered from their catalog. The company was so proud of its financial standing that it encouraged prospective customers to write to the management at the Hammondsport Branch Bank, which held MECO's funds, in order to verify the firm's reputation. Talk about confident businessmen!

Name Your Brand

With so many different manufacturers building motorcycles in the early 1900s, it should come as no surprise that just as many

Outside the Reading Motorcycle Club's hangout in late 1928. The Reading Motorcycle Club has origins as early as 1905, but didn't officially incorporate until 1914. They eventually bought property on Jefferson Street, in Oley, Pennsylvania, sometime in 1928, and are still very active today. This historic motorcycle club participated in, and promoted all kinds of motorcycle events, including Jack Pine enduros, hill climbs, and speedway racing. Typically, they plan an event to coincide with the Oley-based Antique Motorcycle Club of America's spring meet. This meet is hosted by the Perkiomen Chapter of the AMCA, and is on the grounds of the Oley Fire Department, right next to the property where Reading holds its drag races!

companies were busy inventing every little gadget or accessory that they thought some motorcycle enthusiasts couldn't live without. The turn of the century really was a perfect setting for enterprising people with knowledge of manufacturing processes. One look through the pages of the MECO catalog reveals that any idea remotely related to motorcycling was made into a salable product. Some were worthwhile, and some were not, but if you could think something up, chances were good that it was already in the catalog.

Six pages of the catalog alone were devoted to tires and tire products, including vulcanizing kits, tire patches, air pumps, pressure gauges, tire tools, just to name a few. Many of these products were an absolute necessity to the rider. The soft compound of the tires and the mostly unpaved roads created the perfect formula for tires with little durability. Most riders carried some kind of patch kit or spare tube for emergency use. As many of the photos in this book reveal, tires with tread were the exception, not the rule! The cost of a motorcycle tire in the early 1920s was about $11 for a 26" x 3" tire, with maker names still familiar today, such as Firestone and Goodyear, and several companies that are no longer in business, like the United States Tire Company and Empire Motorcycle Tires.

MECO also carried a wide assortment of Mendenhall's road maps, which claimed to show the best and shortest roads between two points, as well as any important information for each major town. This included such things as railroad locations, hotel accommodations, and other tourist information. The most important

This ghostly image was the result of negative overexposure, but it is still a very interesting shot. Both riders are wearing their caps backward, and sport the essential leg puttees and goggles.

thing that any rider really wanted to know, was where to buy gasoline in each town. This information greatly outweighed which hotel had the best food. Although some map makers began printing maps in the late 1800s during the peak years of the bicycling craze, many of the maps offered for sale in the early teens lacked current information about new roads and landmarks. As motor vehicle use increased at an ever-growing rate, the construction of new roads grew at the same pace, making maps useless just months after they were printed.

Let There Be Light!

For the adventurous rider, darkness was no reason to stop riding for the day. With this in mind, MECO offered a wide assortment of motorcycle lighting devices in their catalog. By the year 1915, both Harley-Davidson and Indian offered electric models equipped with lighting, as an option, of course. Harley-Davidson machines used a gear-driven magneto manufactured by the Remy Electric Corporation, which had already established a network of service to support repairs and replacements. The Indian Motorcycle Company even boasted a model equipped with electric start in 1914, but the twin batteries needed charging overnight, and the machine proved to be impractical for daily use. In spite of the fact that electrically equipped motorcycles were becoming more common, many riders still preferred acetylene lamps. These lamps had to be lit with matches, and required the use of a gas tank to supply the lamp. The tanks themselves became well known by one of the makers' names, and were usually referred to as "Prest-O-Lite" tanks. A tank full of acetylene gas was good for about 40 hours of light under good conditions. No one was completely sure what these conditions were, so you had to hope for the best! Leaky fittings and lines shortened the useful life span of a tank of gas, and little by little, riders became more eager to try machines with electric equipment. The depleted tanks could be exchanged at various shops and garages for a full one, much as we would exchange a propane tank for our barbecue grill today.

Many of the items offered for sale through catalogs were components that came as original equipment on the better machines. Parts such as Corbin speedometers, Schebler carburetors, Mesinger and Persons saddles, were all available through MECO and other mail order firms. This way, even if you didn't own one of the big-name machines, you could at least equip your machine like one of them through the pages of a catalog. There is no evidence to support or refute claims that the dealers disliked the mail order houses, but they must have put a dent in the dealer's business. Motorcyclists had the ability to shop from home without visiting their local dealer, and MECO made sure that the experience was a pleasant one for its customers. For many rural riders, mail order was the only way to purchase accessories for their machines, because the distance to a motorcycle shop or dealer was too far to travel for parts and accessories.

Toys and Necessities

Among the strangest of the many items listed in the MECO catalog was the MECO "Rider's firearm," a six-shot, .22 calibre revolver that sold for $4.95. It was said to be indispensable for getting rid of annoying dogs, and to help the cyclist feel secure anywhere he might travel. In those days, gun control evidently meant being able to hit a vicious dog at twenty yards! For those riders still stuck with a belt-drive machine, there were replacement belts and belt dressing, and most important of all, there was leather cement for repairing your belt when it broke apart in the middle of nowhere.

An example of the competition. By 1930, the only serious contender for Harley-Davidson's market was Indian. This Chief was owned by Plummer Wiley, who also owned a Harley. Like many motorcyclists of the era, he found it necessary to try out different brands to determine which was best. This machine is also well equipped, with tandem seat, leather saddlebags, lighted speedometer, and spot lamps. Even though this particular rider had several models from each manufacturer, he preferred the Indians to Harley-Davidson.

If you happened to own an older machine that was showing its age from chipped paint or faded decals, MECO carried everything you needed to refurbish your machine, from air-drying enamel in the original colors, to the exact reproductions of the manufacturer's decals to put on the tank.

If you were in the market for a sidecar for your machine, then you need look no farther than the pages of the MECO catalog to find one. Four different models of Rogers sidecars were listed for prices ranging from $115 to $140. For an additional $5, an extension axle could be ordered for your new sidecar, allowing you the ability to change the track width of your rig to match the ruts in the road made by automobiles. This made for easier going on country roads.

Have Bike, Will Ship!

Many small dealers and shops advertised in some of the more popular trade publications of the day, such as *Motorcycling and Bicycling Magazine,* to buy or sell used machines. Often these ads would be headlined with the eye-catching phrase, "Motorcycles, $5." Even in the back pages of *Popular Mechanics* magazine, such ads could be found. These dealers, or agencies, as some were called, bought and refurbished older machines before listing them for sale in their ads. Although there was a chance that someone might pick up a good deal through these agencies, chances were greater that you would wind up buying a machine that was no longer made, or was in poor condition. Without the benefit of a warranty or service to repair these machines, many buyers were left walking after a short time. Such were the perils of mail order motorcycling!

Some of the boys in the West Hartford, Connecticut, neighborhood that Plummer Wiley lived in. Plum, as his friends called him, was definitely obsessed with motorcycles and motorcycle events. He owned dozens of Harleys, Indians, and Hendersons over a period of about ten years. Plum is at far left in this photo. The two Harleys are flanked by Indians on both sides.

MOTORCYCLE EQUIPMENT CO. **MECO** **HAMMONDSPORT, N.Y. LOS ANGELES, CAL.**

THE FINEST QUALITY PUTTEES AT THE LOWEST POSSIBLE PRICES

Our line of Puttees is by far the best we have ever been able to offer our customers. We anticipated the large demand for puttees and were fortunate enough to secure a tremendous stock before leather advanced to its present high price. A comparison of the prices named below with those quoted by other houses, quality considered, will convince you that we are giving our customers the advantage of the low price we paid.

Please remember, WE DO NOT STOCK EITHER SECONDS OR IMITATION LEATHER PUT-TEES OR LEGGINGS. We give you only the best and if after receiving a pair of our puttees, you feel that you have not received the worth of your money, return them at once, undamaged, and we will cheerfully and promptly refund your money. We can freely make this offer because we know and believe in the puttees we are offering you.

143-157-258   **230**   **105**   **PD**

ALWAYS STATE SIZE—Give in inches loose measurement around calf over trousers.

PUTTEE NO. 143—$7.50 per pair—This moulded puttee is absolutely the best one on the market for the reason that none better can be made. Heavy smooth grain tan leather, thoroughly reinforced and well stitched along top, front and bottom. This is the puttee that is worn by army officers and is the identical one for which city stores are asking $9.

PUTTEE NO. 143C—$7.50 per pair—The same as No. 143 except that the color is chocolate.

PUTTEE No. 157—$7.00 per pair—A genuine pigskin puttee of chocolate color. Fully reinforced and securely stitched along top, front and bottom. Has heavy ¾ in. single wrap strap and the popular adjustable loop fastener at top. Very neat in appearance and will give the best of service.

PUTTEE NO. 258—$7.25 per pair—A one-piece moulded puttee made of best grade of smooth grain cordovan leather, color mahogany. Faced and firmly stitched along top, front and bottom.

PUTTEE NO. 230—$4.75 per pair—A one-piece moulded puttee made of selected smooth finished cowhide, color mahogany. Fully reinforced along top, front and bottom. Has the popular spring front fastening.

PUTTEE NO. 105—$4.25 per pair—A one-piece moulded puttee made of selected, smooth finished leather. Unlined. Excellent value for the money.

PUTTEE NO. PD—$1.30 per pair—We have had this puttee specially made for us to meet the large demand for a canvas puttee of the U. S. Army style. It is made of heavy canvas, nicely formed to fit the leg, and so constructed that it will not wrinkle down. It has a very neat appearance in every way. The amount of wear in these puttees will surprise you.

CORBIN PAD LOCK

No. F15 Price, 25c
A handy lock with two keys to use for many purposes besides locking the motorcycle or accessories you do not wish stolen. Length of loop, 1¼ in.

MECO MENDSALL CEMENT

No. C46 —15c

This cement sticks permanently, wood, glass, furniture, china, leather, bone, celluloid, metal, cloth or any article where an extra strong cement is required. It is water and fire proof. Never leaks where mended. A wonderful article.

TRANSFERS

These motorcycle transfers are exact duplicates of the ones used on the Indian, H. D. and Excelsior. If you have occasion to enamel your machine or if your transfers become scratched or marred, it is very desirable to obtain new ones. It has also become a very popular idea for the rider to have his initials in small letters on the tank or tool box of his machine. The ones we stock are block letters ¾ in. in height, with gilt body and narrow black border which makes a very neat appearance on any color of enamel.

No. G31—Indian tank transfer......................each 18c
No. G35—Harley Davidson tank transfer...........each 18c
No. G39—Harley Davidson tool box transfer.......each 10c
No. G41—Excelsior tank transfer ....each 18c
No. G43—Excelsior small trade mark...............each 10c
No. G45—Initial letter transfer..................each 5c

View from above. This look down on a 1929 Harley-Davidson clearly shows the dual headlamps that Harley used for two years only, 1929 and 1930. The auxiliary spotlight and tandem seat make this machine very well equipped for the time. Proud owner, twenty-year-old Plummer Wiley is dressed for riding with leather helmet and goggles, and wide leather kidney belt wrapped around his sweater. The kidney belt took some of the jolt out of bad roads. The front brake lever is located on the lefthand side of the bars. The bike has a Connecticut tag bearing the single digit "2." Did Plummer perhaps know someone high up at the MVA?

Winter riding in Connecticut. Two chums out for a cold ride on their respective mounts. At back is a 1928 Indian Chief with the Princess sidecar, a $100 option from Indian. In front is a 1928 Harley-Davidson in a popular color choice of white. Both bikes sport auxiliary spotlights to supplement their slightly inadequate headlamps.

MECO STEEL BALLS

Highest Grade

		Per Pkg. of 25	Per Pkg. of 100
No. A1F,	1/8-in.	$0.10	$0.27
No. A2F,	5/32-in.	.11	.32
No. A3F,	3/16-in.	.13	.36
No. A4F,	1/4-in.	.19	.51
No. A5F,	5/16-in.	.29	.77
No. A6F,	3/8-in.	.45	1.20
No. A7F,	7/16-in.	.72	2.15
No. A8F,	1/2-in.	1.00	3.10

STAR BALL RETAINER

The merit of Star Ball Retainers is known by everyone as they have been on the market for years. They are used in practically every important bearing on a motorcycle. The prices given below include the balls. Some others list them without balls at these prices.

STAR BALL RETAINERS FOR MOTORCYCLES

Order by our Stock Number

STAR BALL RETAINERS USED IN INDIAN MOTORCYCLES

Our Stock No.	Indian Cat. No.		Balls	Diam.	Cup Size	Price Each
23	A13090x	Front Wheel 1909 and 1910	8	1/4 in.	1 3/16 in.	20c
60	C13090x	Front Wheel 1911 to 1915	7	1/4 in.	1 1/4 in.	20c
97	A25190x	Large Retainer Corbin Brake 1909 to 1915	8	3/8 in.	1 11/16 in.	25c
34	A25200x	Small Retainer Corbin Brake 1909 to 1915	7	5/16 in.	1 11/16 in.	20c
70	C18205	Countershaft 1911 to 1915	14	1/4 in.	1 11/16 in.	40c
6		Splitdorf Magneto Shaft 1914	7	3/16 in.	3/4 in.	15c

STAR BALL RETAINERS USED IN EXCELSIOR MOTORCYCLES

Our No.	Ex. No.		Balls	Diam.	Cup Size	Price Each
97	138	Large Ball Retainer, Corbin Brake	8	3/8 in.	1 11/16 in.	25c
34	139	Small Ball Retainer, Corbin Brake	7	5/16 in.	1 11/16 in.	20c
115	LL 16	Large Ball Retainer, 1914 New Departure Brake	10	3/16 in.	2 5/16 in.	45c
47	LL 20	Small Ball Retainer, 1914 New Departure Brake	7	3/8 in.	1 1/2 in.	30c
67		Large Ball Retainer, 1912-13 New Departure Brake	8	3/8 in.	1 11/16 in.	30c
34		Small Ball Retainer, 1912-13 New Departure Brake	7	5/16 in.	1 11/16 in.	20c
97	3656	Large Ball Retainer, Musselman Brake	8	3/8 in.	1 11/16 in.	25c
97	3656	Split Ball Retainer, Musselman Brake	8	3/8 in.	1 11/16 in.	25c
47	3661	Small Ball Retainer, Musselman Brake	7	3/8 in.	1 1/2 in.	30c
23	3672	Front Hub Retainer	8	1/4 in.	1 3/16 in.	20c
139	2192	Large Retainer, Two Speed Gear	18	5/16 in.	3 in.	45c
100	2193	Intermediate Retainer, Two Speed Gear	13	5/16 in.	2 3/16 in.	40c
87	2194	Small Retainer, Two Speed Gear	12	5/16 in.	2 1/32 in.	35c

STAR BALL RETAINER USED IN HARLEY-DAVIDSON MOTORCYCLES

Our No.	H-D No.		Balls	Diam.	Cup Size	Price Each
23	D5	Front Hub Retainer	8	1/4 in.	1 3/16 in.	20c
66	BF119	Right Cone Retainer, Disc Brake	10	5/16 in.	1 11/16 in.	25c
ZZ	DG562	Special Clutch Thrust. All 3 speeds	9	1/4 in.	1 1/4 in.	25c
C	DG176	Clutch Thrust. All 2 speeds	8	1/4 in.	1 1/16 in.	25c

STAR BALL RETAINERS USED IN ECLIPSE CLUTCHES AND COASTER BRAKES

Excelsior Use Same Numbers in Their Catalogue

Our No.	Eclipse No.		Balls	Diam.	Cup Size	Price Each
OO	CP13	Thrust Balls and Retainers	14	1/4 in.	2 in.	50c
F	CH10	Internal Thrust Retainer	13	1/4 in.	1 11/16 in.	50c
170	CH13	Outer Thrust Retainer	14	1/4 in.	1 11/16 in.	50c
66	BB14	Small Retainer, Adjusting Cone	10	5/16 in.	1 11/16 in.	25c
23	K5	Front Hub Retainer	8	1/4 in.	1 3/16 in.	20c
RR		Star Ball Retainer for Corbin-Brown Speedometer Shaft	8	3/16 in.	11/16 in.	15c
6		Star Ball Retainer for Splitdorf Motorcycle Magneto	7	3/16 in.	3/4 in.	15c

MECO RIDER'S FIREARM

No. C104—Price, $4.95

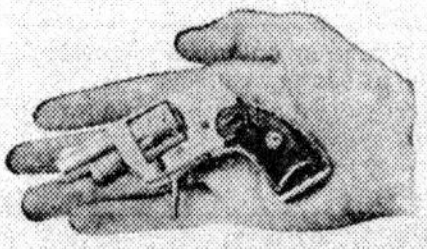

Every rider one or more times in a lifetime needs a protector. The Meco Firearm makes you feel secure any place because you know you possess a hard-hitting, 6-shot, 22 Cal. revolver that you can depend on. For vicious, annoying dogs it is indispensable. It is nicely nickel plated and fully guaranteed. Weighs only 6 ozs. and fits snugly in the hip or side pocket of a motorcycle suit where a long-barreled revolver could not be carried. Sporting goods stores ask $6.00 for this quality firearm. Has folding trigger.

Note: New York State residents will have to submit their permit before we can ship. The permit will be returned at once. These permits can be obtained from your County Judge.

SAFETY KEY RING

No. B33—15c

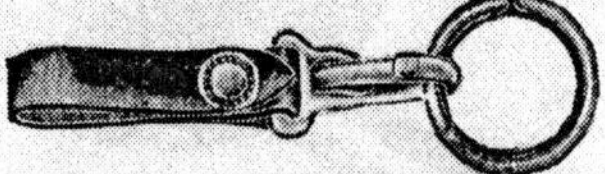

A strong nickel-plated key ring with snap fastener and leather loop for attaching to your belt. The snap permits the ring to be instantly detached. The use of this little article prevents the common annoyance caused by lost or misplaced keys.

WRIST SUPPORTER

No. B51—25c

A pliable, leatherette wrist band, lined with thick, soft felt. Has double straps and is built to give both service and comfort to the user. Usually sold for 50c.

The homemade sidecar rig on this Chief is doing its duty. Hauling another bike was what owner Plummer Wiley had in mind when he added this box to his 1927 Indian Chief. Its 74-cubic-inch displacement had plenty of power to haul the sidecar and its contents.

Chester G. Wiley, and his son, Plummer Wiley, pose with two of their automobiles and one of Plummer's many motorcycles in front of their Connecticut home. Earlier in the year, Chester and his son logged over 12,000 miles through 30 states in the Model A Ford station wagon in the middle. They also traveled through Canada and Mexico, collecting automobile license plates on the trip home.

Plum Wiley tries to clear out the oil in the lower end of his Chief engine on a snowy day in West Hartford, Connecticut. Engine lubrication was "constant loss" on early machines, meaning that every so many miles, the engine crankcases had to be drained, or else this would happen.

SPRINGTIME is get-together-time — out of doors! You enjoy old friends more — make new friends — and pack every outdoor hour with pleasure — when you own a 1936 Harley-Davidson. . . It's some motorcycle! You'll marvel at its wind-piercing lines and perfect balance — its airplane-like speed and snap — and above all, the amazing performance of its up-to-the-minute motor with new and exclusive features. Many sparkling color combinations— every one a beauty. Streamlined sidecar or chummy "Buddy Seat" for get-together rides—available on the 45's, 74's and the new 80 cubic inch Twin.

See your nearest Harley-Davidson dealer—PRONTO! Ask him for a FREE RIDE—about his EASY PAY PLANS — and *send in the coupon.*

MAIL THIS COUPON

HARLEY-DAVIDSON MOTOR CO.
Dept.-F, Milwaukee, Wis.
Send colorful folder illustrating and describing the 1936 models. Postage stamp is enclosed to cover cost of mailing.

Name...
Address...
My age is □ 16-19 years, □ 20-30 years, □ 31 years and up, □ under 16 years. Check your age group.

When writing to advertisers please mention Popular Mechanics

with a
HARLEY-DAVIDSON

Everywhere riders are "winging" to new and enchanting scenes
—making the most of glorious fall days. You, too, can see more ot
the country in its reds, browns, and golden yellow coloring—from the saddle of a Harley-Davidson! Low-cost mileage—flashing style—speed like you are
on wing — those are the thrills that are yours with Harley-Davidson streamline
design and latest motor improvements. Get your Harley-Davidson now—and go
"flying high" with those other happy Harley-Davidson riders in your town!
See your Harley-Davidson dealer RIGHT AWAY — for a *free* ride — and
details of his Easy-Pay Plans. And send in the coupon — Now!

Harley-Davidson Motor Co., Dept. P,   Milwaukee, Wis.

Ride a
HARLEY-
DAVIDSON

HARLEY-DAVIDSON MOTOR CO.,
Dept. P, Milwaukee, Wis.
Interested in motorcycling. Send illustrated literature. Stamp is enclosed to
cover mailing cost.

Name...

Address..
My age is ☐ 16-19 years, ☐ 20-30
years, ☐ 31 years and up, ☐ under 16
years. Check your age groups

This rear view of Plum Wiley's 1930 Model DL Harley-Davidson shows off his coveted No. 2 Connecticut license tag. Plum acquired this tag by requesting the lowest possible number each year, and in the year prior to this photo, he finally got this tag. He was able to keep this low number for the next ten years, and still owned the metal tag when I met him in 1991.

Side shot of Plum's 1930 Harley-Davidson Model DL. This machine was a 45-cubic-inch side valve flathead, equipped with a three-speed transmission. The small twin headlights were used for two years on the H-D motorcycles, 1929 and 1930. The lamps were inadequate for road use, and often were mistaken for the two headlights of a car far away. In 1931, the Motor Company went back to a single headlight. This photo was taken in 1933.

HARLEY-DAVIDSON
MOTORCYCLES

Lots of style—fast get-away—zooming speed—power galore —and a gliding ride that's smooth and trouble-free. Sure thing—these streamlined 1937 Harley-Davidsons are ruggedly built—have perfect balance—instant response of power when driving conditions demand—and dependable brakes both front and rear for quick, easy stops... Yes, plenty of thrills—go where you will—get there quickly, safely and economically in the saddle of a 1937 Harley-Davidson... See your nearest Harley-Davidson Dealer RIGHT AWAY. Take a FREE ride on a 1937 Harley-Davidson — ask about his Easy Pay Plans. And send in the coupon.

Ride a —

HARLEY-DAVIDSON

Another lineup of the West Hartford boys, showing Plum's homemade pickup sidecar, which had to be handy for bringing broken-down machines back home. No doubt Plum was popular with all his riding buddies. Two of these bikes sport accessory spotlights. These spots were a common add-on to supplement the original equipment lamps. The aviator-type leather helmets were also well liked by motorcyclists, especially those who rode in colder climates.

Plum Wiley on his Henderson next to his father's house in Connecticut. The bike had new rubber front and rear, enough for a summer's worth of good riding! This machine was also equipped with a tandem seat behind the operator, so Plum could bring a friend along! The four-cylinder engine had plenty of power to pull a passenger and still deliver great gas mileage.

Plum's dad, Chester Wiley, takes a spin on this 1930 DL Harley. I'm not quite sure what the bundle of weeds is on the front fender, but perhaps they were hoping it would improve the traction of the almost bald front tire. The small, twin headlights are very visible, at least in the daylight! A Klaxon horn is nestled between the lamps, with a round toolbox just below it.

FOR LOW COST **SPORT**

RIDE A 1937 **HARLEY-DAVIDSON**

Harley-Davidsons have always been easy on the pocketbook—but the new 1937 models take mileage costs to new low levels!

The answer is in the new improved Harley-Davidson motors with their many advanced features. Circulating pressure oiling—roller bearings throughout—improved cooling—four speeds forward—external ignition timer—all spell increased gas and oil mileage.

Greater economy, SURE — but that's only the beginning! You have to see and ride one of the 1937 Harley-Davidsons to get the real thrill of their classy lines, snappy colors—their double loop trussed frames, welded steel saddle-type tanks—and built-in instrument panel with its 120 M.P.H. speedometer dial!

See your nearest Harley-Davidson dealer NOW—take a FREE ride on one of the new models—ask about his Easy Pay Plans. And send in the coupon.

Los Angeles, Oct. 9th—News Flash—Bill Connelly and Fred Dauria cross continent from New York City in fastest time ever made by motorcycle. Their record—69 hours 46 minutes—beats former sidecar record by 17 hours 9 minutes. Exceeds best previous solo time by 1 hour 34 minutes. Their sidecar outfit—a Harley-Davidson—of course!

Ride a **HARLEY-DAVIDSON**

HARLEY-DAVIDSON MOTOR CO.
Dept. P,   Milwaukee, Wis.
Interested in motorcycling. Send illustrated literature. Postage stamp is enclosed to cover mailing cost.

Name...
Address...
My age is ☐ 16-19 years, ☐ 20-30 years, ☐ 31 years and up, ☐ under 16 years. Check your age group.

When writing to advertisers please mention Popular Mechanics

THE DYNAMIC NEW 74 TWIN

THE SPORTY NEW 45 TWIN

CPSIA information can be obtained at www.ICGtesting.com
Printed in the USA
BVOW02*0827050115

381583BV00051B/470/P

9 781630 263522